Soldier or Scholar

Stratocles or War

Soldier or SCHOLAR
Stratocles or War

Jacobus Pontanus

Translated by
Caitlin Allender
Michael Campitelli
Caitlin Engler
Richard Gibbons
Sean Gloth
Elida Lynch
Irene Murphy
Nathan Zawie

Contributions by
Katherine Bagley
Lorraine Cuddeback
Mark Meleka
Michael Mennis
Alexander Vaeth
Ashley Woodworth

Edited, with appendices and contributions by
Thomas D. McCreight
Paul Richard Blum

Apprentice House
Baltimore, Maryland
www.ApprenticeHouse.com

Printed in the United States of America

First Edition

ISBN: 978-1-934074-48-0

Published by Apprentice House
The Future of Publishing...Today!

Apprentice House
Communication Department
Loyola University Maryland
4501 N. Charles Street
Baltimore, MD 21210

410.617.5265 • 410.617.5040 (fax)
www.ApprenticeHouse.com • info@ApprenticeHouse.com

Acknowledgements

There are always many people to thank when a project bears fruit; when the project is large and multidisciplinary like this one, we feel a greater need. Without the support of Loyola's Center for Humanities and its Director Claire Mathews-McGuiness this would not have been possible. Dean of Arts and Sciences James Buckley lent his support, along with Loyola's Program in Catholic Studies under the direction of Angela Christman. We owe a debt of gratitude to the editorial board of Apprentice House for approving and nurturing this book. The Interlibrary Loan department of the Loyola-Notre Dame Library helped us out often, and quickly, as did Lisa Flaherty, Administrative Assistant in the department of Philosophy. The departments of Philosophy and of Classics made space in their schedules and budgets for an interdisciplinary project and a team-taught course that undergirded the entire enterprise. They also supplied enthusiastic and critical audiences, composed of both students and faculty, for readings at various times of parts (or the whole) of the translation. Kevin Atticks and his cohorts at Apprentice House offered moral and practical support and sage advice at many stages, most importantly during the final ones.

Many thanks are owed to many friends for reading different versions of many parts of this effort. Robert Miola of the English department gave us good advice, and he and his students supplied us with an admirable model of how to execute a project like this one. We offer special thanks to Professor Ulrich Leinsle of the University of Regensburg, not only for his extensive and clearly presented research on topics relevant to our task, but especially for supplying us with images of a manuscript that allowed us to improve both the text and the translation of the play here translated.

Our principal gratitude is owed to Joseph Walsh of the Classics department. Professor Walsh produced the first volume in this series of texts by and for undergraduates, and now chairs the editorial board that decides what projects to pursue. Many of the students who were involved in the maiden voyage of this series also participated in the present volume, and their experience was invaluable as we proceeded.

The following is a hackneyed conceit, but true nonetheless: despite all the help we received, the errors remaining in this volume must properly be attributed to its editors. We thank everyone involved for their encouragement and assistance, and ask indulgence for the mistakes that remain.

$\mathcal{T}able\ of\ \mathcal{C}ontents$

Illustrations

P. 2, 9, and 161: Decorative vignettes from 16th century prints.

P. 4: Public announcement of a disputation for graduation of six students of Jacobus Pontanus (Dillingen 1577; Leinsle, *Disputationes* 2006).

P. 10: Portrait of Jacobus Pontanus.

P. 20: Title page of the first Dillingen print of Ignatius's *Spiritual Exercises* (1582).

P. 26: Schoolyard of the Jesuit School in Dillingen (1627).

P. 34: College and church of St. Salvator in Augsburg (1679).

P. 46: Title page of Pontanus' commentary on Virgil (1599).

P. 50: Beginning of *Stratocles* in the manuscript M2 (see above p. 53); courtesy of Ulrich G. Leinsle, Regensburg.

P. 58: A soldier and a sutler on the title page of a Jesuit play by Jacobus Balde (1604-68).

P. 164 and 173: Good students and bad students in *The School of Christ* and *The School of Satan* from a booklet of moral examples, Munich 1618.

P. 167: Title page of a philosophy disputation Ingolstadt 1636 of Leodegard Hertenstein, S.J.

Except for pages 4 and 50, all illustrations are taken from Duhr vols. I and II.

Preface

As we write this, wars rage in many parts of the globe. In all the various conflicts, the forces on both sides are drawn primarily from young people of high school or college age (and sometimes younger). Many soldiers return from combat convinced of the value and rightness of their wars, but many also return disillusioned and traumatized by the very real savagery of modern combat. Even worse, the toll on the ground among the civilian population is severe. Such is the state of contemporary warfare, waged by those who could be, and sometimes are, students.

The play translated in this volume confronts problems and questions similar to our own, but from a gap of over four centuries. Should students fight? Which ones? Why? Why not? What role should teachers play in students' decision to enlist? What about the desires and claims of family and loved ones? What are the claims of the state on its youth? How ready are young people to make decisions of this magnitude? How are the views of veterans to be weighed? All these important questions are raised in this play. We hope to offer a document of student life in the sixteenth century that also stimulates reflection on these issues that, unfortunately, are not bound by time and continue to be relevant.

Decorative vignette from a 16th century print.

Introduction

Public announcement of a disputation for graduation of six students of Jacobus Pontanus (Dillingen 1577; Leinsle, *Disputationes* 2006). The theses to be defended were: In Political Sciences: Who is more apt to live a happy life: a king or a citizen? In Economics: Should youth study abroad? In Ethics: Is it possible to praise oneself? Is it possible to love one's enemies even in politics? In Physics: What is more useful: water or fire? Can the void be coherent in things?

How to use this book

This book is a hybrid intended for use by different audiences. On the one hand, we hope to make Neo Latin literature accessible to modern undergraduates. Students who study Latin nowadays seldom have access, even at the graduate level, to recent editions with commentary of works from this large and important portion of extant Latin literature.[1] On the other hand, since a good reading knowledge of Latin is rare among today's pupils, we want to put in their hands a good, clear, readable translation of some of the vast and historically significant literature that was produced in Latin in the early modern period. This is especially true for literature that has contemporary relevance: in a time of war, this is a play about war and how students should think about war and its effects on themselves and others. To that end we have produced a book with a Latin text and a facing English translation.

1. There has been recent improvement in the availability of Neo Latin texts, principally but not only on the Internet. The Harvard University Series *I Tatti Renaissance Library* is putting out good editions of important pieces. On the Internet there are some very large repositories of different types of texts and bibliographies. We mention here only the ones we have found most useful: for Neo Latin Drama especially, Dana Sutton's *Philological Museum* at http://www.philological.bham.ac.uk/bibliography/; for material primarily from the German-speaking (now or earlier) areas of Europe, *Mateo* (University of Mannheim texts on-line), especially the section called *Camena*, at http://www.uni-mannheim. de/mateo/; *Neo-Latin Colloquia*, started by the late Ross Scaife, updated by Terence Tunberg, that focuses on Neo Latin instructional texts, http://www.stoa.org/colloquia/anglice.shtml.

Text: Line Numbers

We print the Latin text from Rädle's 1979 critical edition with a facing German translation (Rädle 1979). Where our text differs from his, we indicate in the notes the reasons for preferring a given reading to what he prints. We preserve his line numbering with one important exception, to be discussed below. The numbers in the facing English translation correspond with the Latin line numbers, and in this prose translation we have been able to line them up closely. We have done this for two reasons: both to simplify reference and comparison between the Latin and English versions, and also to make the explanatory endnotes accessible for readers who read Latin as well as those who do not (see our section below on Notes).

Regarding our departure from Rädle's line numbering: As will be discussed below in the sections on Jesuit Drama and History of the Text, this play was performed in different versions at different times. One of the versions was intended for a Mardi Gras performance (the Tuesday before Ash Wednesday, the beginning of Lent). On that day there was more freedom to include otherwise morally suspect material, and in this version we find, for instance, long sections with a feisty female character named Faustina, plenty of slapstick between her and her estranged husband, lots of double entendres, and both open and thinly veiled references to drinking, gambling and sex. The manuscript with these pieces also includes notes indicating where in the older version this new material was to be inserted. Rädle published these parts as an appendix in different sections. We believe the play holds together quite well with these portions included; it deepens some otherwise flat characters, and it makes the play much more amusing for a modern audience. We thus have produced a running text with all of Rädle's appendix entries included where Pontanus indicated. We have also preserved Rädle's line numbering of these smaller sections in order to facilitate comparison between the two versions produced by Pontanus. We thus have running line numbers, but where a portion is inserted from the "Mardi

Gras" version, we number that section as, e.g. "A.2", where "A" indicates that this is an appendix entry in Rädle's edition, and "2" indicates the second of those sections. Line numbers within those sections are numbered beginning from one.

Translation

We wanted to produce a version that would be close enough to the original to be useful for students of Latin but also fluent and idiomatic enough to be attractive to modern readers who do not read Latin. Compromise, substitution and approximation are necessary in every translation; we hope to have produced a version that is readable and performable in addition to being relatively faithful to the original. Some examples of our decisions are the following:

We have used modern names for countries, for example, instead of the designations current in sixteenth century Latin. On the other hand, we have not substituted modern names of famous generals or wars. Where a pun appears in the Latin, we have attempted to render one in English; if the attempt to do so produced strained language, we fell back on a more literal rendering and included an endnote about the play on words. Where the Latin has alliteration or assonance, we have attempted the same. In one instance (29) a character quotes Greek, and we elected to render it with a simple French phrase. Pontanus on occasion uses tragic or lofty diction and archaic vocabulary for (sometimes) emotional or (often) comic effect. Where he does so, we have tried to retain that flavor in the English, employing dated word order and the occasional "thou". Pontanus is fond of proverbs and sayings, but in almost every instance he introduces them with a prefatory note like "as the saying goes" or something similar. This made our work much easier, since he (no doubt for the benefit of his students who were trying to learn Latin partly by learning and performing his plays) makes the proverbial nature of the material clear to the listener.

In one instance we quote the Latin in the text and then

translate it (219). This proverb was also the title of a piece by Erasmus about war to which the play is heavily indebted, so we though it best to single that out for special treatment (**Bellum dulce est inexpertis**, "War is sweet to those without experience (of it)"). Especially in the dialogue sections where the Latin is more informal, we have used contractions like "it's" or "I've" in order to convey a conversational tone. The exception to this is the character Eubulus, the teacher, whose Latin is more formal, archaic and allusive, and whose English we felt should therefore be more proper and strict.

Notes

We elected to use endnotes in order to present uncluttered pages and a translation relatively free of distractions and interruptions. The notes are designed for use both by readers of Latin and those who cannot read the language, and combine material of potential interest to both groups. They are keyed to the English translation but include the line number in the Latin text and the Latin word or phrase as well as the English word or phrase to be commented on. In descending order of frequency, the notes are of the following types:

Comments on the translation, with remarks on any textual issues or other possible ways to translate the passage, along with observations on the thematic import or relation to other similar passages in the play.

Explanation of quotations from or allusions to Classical literature. We often include remarks that clarify the significance of a given allusion to the immediate context and to the work as a whole. See the introductory section on Pontanus' use of Classical authors for more specifics.

Elucidation of recondite material. This is mainly of two types: explanation of references to Classical places, gods, heroes or events, and of references to historical events, places or people contemporary with Pontanus.

Explanation of quotations from or allusions to Erasmus. Pontanus makes frequent reference to some of Erasmus' works on war, and is fond of quoting from his *Adages*, Erasmus' collection of sayings and proverbs.

Discussion of theological or philosophical questions and problems that were current in Pontanus' time and are alluded to in the play.

Explanation of references to the normal academic life of the students in Pontanus' school, who comprised both the acting company and the chief audience for his dramas.

The abbreviations used in the notes are from the *Oxford Latin Dictionary*, which we refer to as OLD throughout.

Decorative vignette from a 16th century print.

P. Jakob Pontan.

Portrait of Jacobus Pontanus.

Jacobus Pontanus: Biography

Jacobus Pontanus was born Jakob Spanmüller in 1542 in Brüx in Bohemia (now the town of Most in the Czech Republic). The name of his birthplace connotes "bridge"; hence, when he chose a Latin name for himself, as was the fashion for those who saw themselves as "humanists", he named himself "Pontanus" ("from Bridge").[1] Pontanus was educated at the Jesuit Colleges of Prague (Bohemia) and Ingolstadt (Bavaria) and entered the Society of Jesus in 1563. From 1570 through 1579 he taught Humanities and Rhetoric at the Jesuit College in Dillingen (Bavaria). These two classes of the Jesuit curriculum educated students in mastering Latin by reading Classical authors and by offering graduated instruction and practice in elegant writing and speaking. During this period Pontanus wrote the first version of his *Stratocles* and other plays. He also taught Philosophy in the years 1572-73 and 1576-79 in Dillingen.

After having been appointed *magister perpetuus* (tenured instructor) he was engaged in founding the Jesuit school St. Salvator in Augsburg, and in the year 1582 he began work there as the dean of Poetry and Rhetoric. As a new school, St. Salvator was in direct competition for students with the nearby Protestant school, St. Anna, and one method of attracting students was the production of plays. In 1586 he became a member of the

---

1. Sources for this short biography are: Leinsle 2005 and 2009; Blum 1993; Boehm 1982; Pontanus 1979 (Rädle); Janssen 1906; Specht 1902; de Backer/Sommervogel 1895.

committee that evaluated the preliminary version of the Jesuit curriculum, known as *Ratio Studiorum*, to which he submitted suggestions for revision regarding the humanities (see Appendix on Humanistic Studies). This document came to be the most important source for the constitution of Jesuit schools across the globe. Pontanus' influence on its generation testifies to his importance as an educational theorist and practitioner.

As a philologist, a master of both the Latin and Greek languages, he wrote lengthy, learned and respected commentaries on Vergil and Ovid, and the multivolume *Progymnasmata Latinitatis*. This was his most famous and influential work and continued to be used even in Protestant schools all the way into the 1700s. The title of the work means "Preliminary or Warm-up Exercises in Latin"; it consisted of a series of dialogues in excellent but simple Latin intended to give instruction on acquiring mastery of the language, both in conversation and in writing. Pontanus also wrote many Latin plays intended for student performance on subjects selected from the Bible and from ancient history; these were designed to give the students a hands-on approach to their Latin studies. He was also the author of an influential treatise on rhetoric, *Poeticarum Institutionum Libri Tres*, "Three books on Methods for Teaching Poetry", which was first published in 1594; its 1600 edition contains the final version of the *Stratocles*. Jacobus Pontanus died on November 25, 1626 in Augsburg.

Jesuit Comedy – Seriously?

What place did comedies like *Stratocles* have in Jesuit education during the early formation of the order? What role, if any, did such performances play in enhancing and presenting the message of the Jesuits to their public or private audiences? In order to achieve some understanding of the function of comedic performances such as *Stratocles* in Jesuit education during the time of Jacobus Pontanus, one can review various documents and correspondence related to the issue that were generated by Jesuits around the time of Pontanus' life. These sources were collected in the last century in the *Monumenta Paedagogica Societatis Iesu* (pedagogical documents of the Society of Jesus, cited as *MPSI*)

The multi-volume *Monumenta* contain many Jesuit-authored letters and commentaries on Jesuit teaching practices dating back to the foundation of the order in 1540, including several drafts of the *Ratio Studiorum* (the official rules of Jesuit education) and the final version published in 1599. Among these entries is a thread of remarks written by various administrators on theatrical productions. The sources relating to theater published between 1540 and 1599 are of particular interest because they offer a chronological view of the evolution of comedy in Jesuit educational history leading up to and beyond the premier of Pontanus' play in 1578.

The appearance of theater productions like Pontanus' in Jesuit education should not be surprising, given the order's attraction to ancient culture, including its theater. We see pervasive and extensive presentation of dramas, tragedies and comedies in the history of the Society of Jesus. However, not all Jesuit institutions in Pontanus' time were in agreement on the relevance and utility of theatrical displays. Comedies especially were the topic of much debate among the Jesuits.

Despite this fact, many institutions allowed them space in the curriculum. The purpose of comedic productions was to facilitate the practice of spoken Latin and to make classical literature familiar in a manner that was appealing to students. In many cases the productions also served as opportunities for students to seek financial support. According to Pontanus himself in his 100th dialogue of the *Progymnasmata Latinitatis*, many students who could not pay for their own education attracted benefactors who would pay their tuition for them based on their performance in such events.

The use of comedy in Jesuit education was constrained, however, by several hesitations on the part of Jesuit administrators. According to various sources in the *Monumenta*, many Jesuits restricted the use of theatrical comedy in their desire to preserve the reputable name of the Society of Jesus and Jesuit education, and to avoid instilling impious or distracting notions in their students. These limitations were most likely influenced by a population of Jesuits who disapproved of the use of comedies in their universities altogether.

For instance, one Father Jacobus Philippus Castellano from Bologna, Italy, commented on the matter in 1558, stating that he was embarrassed to be asked by students or townspeople when the next comedy was to be presented. He emphasized that Jesuits must not allow the display of comedies because they were accompanied by undesirable associations for the order (MPSI 3, Mon. 194). Clearly Father Castellano thought comedy was inappropriate and not suited to the aims of Jesuit education.

We see a similar position of disapproval in a statement

issued in the 1570's by the Jesuits in Sardinia in response to a letter sent from the center of the Society in Rome to all Jesuit Provinces inquiring into the circumstances of their respective curricular operations. In their statement, the institution reported that they did not present tragedies or comedies at all because their encouragement of detrimental morals outweighed any perceived benefit (MPSI 4, Mon. 33).

Although such accounts suggest a definitively negative attitude toward comedy in Jesuit education, there are several more remarks in the *Monumenta Paedagogica* that suggest the approval and encouragement of theatrical productions such as comedies. The earliest known accounts of theater productions in Jesuit schools illustrate this position by confirming the presence of dramas and tragedies in early Jesuit education, out of which comedic productions presumably developed.

Included in the *Monumenta* is a chronicle of the history of the Jesuits written in 1574 by Johannes Alphonsus Polanco, Secretary of the Jesuits for three decades. For the year 1555 he recorded that the college of Medina del Campo, in the Valladolid Province of Spain, presented the tragedy of Jephthah (*Judges* 11:34-40) with great success, drawing much applause and advancing the school's reputation. Polanco suggested in his account that the audience's admiration may have been augmented by the fact that the author was a very young man, namely the Jesuit Joseph de Acosta (1540-1600), who had entered the order at the age of 12 (MPSI 1, appendix 1, p. 597). It is also noted that in 1556 a tragedy written by Acosta on the selling of Joseph (*Genesis* 37:12-16) was played in the same town, and another play was staged on Christmas (p. 611).

Further evidence of the early use of theater in the Jesuit tradition is offered in a pair of reports, one from Rome issued in the year 1555, and another from Innsbruck (Austria) issued in 1556. The report from Rome states that a dialogue on how to be reborn with Christ, written by the Jesuit Andreas Frusius (des Freux), was staged in front of a large audience that included a Cardinal and several doctors from Paris (MPSI 1, appendix

1, p. 603). The second report details a comedy with the title *Acolastus* that was set on stage in Innsbruck after Pentecost "with much equipment and the college as proscenium, and not just the walls of the court were decorated but there were also boards and paintings wonderfully adorned; and since the event became public in the town, such a crowd came to the college that not only the courtyard was occupied but also the arcades and upper parts of the building were full of spectators; and through pressure on the guards many entered against our will." (p. 613)

The aforementioned accounts of the first known plays, especially the description of the "first" (of which we are aware) comedic production in Innsbruck, indeed suggest the early employment of comedies in Jesuit education. Later commentaries in the *Monumenta* provide further support for the conclusion that a climate existed in Pontanus' time that encouraged the use of theatrical productions like comedies in the Jesuit curriculum. In particular, there are two Jesuit priests whose remarks serve to summarize the conditions governing the use of comedies for a broad body of the Jesuit institutions existing up to and including Pontanus' time.

Father Paulus Hoffaeus, writing from Prague in 1560, asserted that comedies and other public displays should be put on in an orderly fashion in order to avoid sullying a given school's reputation. Furthermore, Hoffaeus suggested that each of two exam periods be marked by the presentation of a comedy or dialogue by students, one falling on St. Martin's day (early November) at the beginning of the semester, and the other at the conclusion of the second semester around the time of Easter (MPSI 2, Mon. 10).

Father Diego Ledesma, writing from the Collegium Romanum in 1564-1565, authored a chapter on celebrations in which he further discussed the specifics of comedic performances. He recommended that they take place only once a year, at the beginning of each study period, and that they include only student performers in order to preserve the esteemed authority of the priests. Ledesma also emphasized that comedies should not have even the slightest suspicion of indecency but instead be kept pious by excluding any references to pagan gods, maintaining sober language, and involving a serious and edifying theme. Furthermore, women (or men dressed as such) were not to be included in the productions, and any personified virtues or allegories (e.g., the Church, typically referred to as feminine) had to be portrayed by men wearing asexual garments, such as priestly dress. The reason for this rule, according to Ledesma, was to prevent the students (all of whom were boys) from being harmed by the potential scandal suggested by the female figure (MPSI 2, Mon. 76).

The abovementioned regulations offer a reasonable summary of the dominant trends in the role of theatrical comedy in Pontanus' time. Several other documents by Jesuit officials roughly contemporary to Pontanus reflect this fact as well. For instance, it was taken for granted that comedies were presented in Vienna in 1566, according to Jerome Nadal; the limit for production was twice a year (MPSI 3, Mon. 163).

A number of other reports offer a similar position, but are more conservative in their language. For example, a Jesuit institution in Poland reported in 1576 that they generally produce one comedy a year. The conditions for production state that the comedy must be written and performed in Latin, and furthermore, that the work be approved by the Father Provincial (the head of the Jesuit Province in Poland) (MPSI 4, Mon. 34, p. 297). A similar statement issued from Peru in the same year explained that the Jesuit school there rarely performed comedies. However, the report also stated that since comedies were edifying and motivational for students, it was acceptable to perform one comedy a year (in a place where there were no women) to promote educational interests (MPSI 4, Mon. 33, p. 274).

A report by Oliverius Manareus on his visits to German colleges from 1582 to 1586 reflects comparable findings (MPSI 7, Mon. 49, p. 457 f). In summation of his experiences,

Manareus wrote that tragedies and comedies should be played only rarely, unless a prince made an explicit request for one to be presented. It is interesting to note that in some cases the performance of a comedy with a somewhat licentious theme was actually permitted in order to restrain students from more serious sin. For instance, Father Ledesma, as cited earlier, wrote that dialogues and plays should be done only once a year, and before Lent, in order to entice students to remain at school and away from the debauchery awaiting them at local Mardi Gras celebrations. Manareus also referred to *bacchanalia* (or Mardi Gras) performances in his report. Although his focus was on asserting that religious vestments were not to be worn on such occasions, Manareus' account also confirms the fact that comedies were sometimes offered by Jesuit institutions as purportedly healthy alternatives to the potentially sinful activities available to students during Mardi Gras.

From the preceding sources, one can conclude that theater productions including comedies could generally be seen on Jesuit campuses once or twice a year around the time Pontanus' play *Stratocles or War* was produced. Such performances included pious and educational language and themes, and included no women or feminine dress. Their intention was to promote educational interest in students while remaining within the bounds of propriety. One of the early drafts of the *Ratio Studiorum* published in 1586 supports this conclusion in its proclamation that the presentation of comedies is an acceptable way for Jesuits to foster students' interest in their studies (MPSI 5, p. 137).

There is some evidence to suggest that the trend in Pontanus' time was toward a more and more liberal use of theatrical productions in Jesuit education. For instance, theater plays were so well established in Jesuit education in Germany by 1597 that the Jesuits started to print program brochures for their productions that summarized the plot and listed the actors. Although the plays were usually performed in Latin, the programs were typically bilingual (Latin and German) in order to attract a general audience for the public performances.[2] At the same time (early 1600s) it must have become acceptable that public productions were occasionally presented in the vernacular. In Hungary, for instance, the first performance in Hungarian took place in Vágsellye (now in Slovakia) in 1601.[3]

The debate on the role of comedy in Jesuit education does not cease here.[4] Yet it is possible to glean from the sources surveyed above the general climate of Pontanus' time in regard to the nature and use of writings such as *Stratocles* in Jesuit education.

---

2. See Szarota's seven volume collection of these documents.
3. Alszeghy et al. 9.
4. A summary of the position in the 17th century can be found in Juvencius (often listed as Juventius or Jouvancy: 1643-1719) § 5, p. 95 (accessible at
http://www.juntadeandalucia.es/cultura/bibliotecavirtualandalucia)

EXERCITIA
SPIRITVALIA
Ignatij de Loyola.

Cum Facultate Superiorum.

DILINGAE,
Excudebat Joannes Mayer

M.D.LXXXII.

Titelblatt der erſten Dillinger Ausgabe
der Exerzitien 1582. (Originalgröße.)

Title page of the first Dillingen print of Ignatius's *Spiritual Exercises* (1582).

The Stratocles as a Spiritual Exercise

St. Ignatius Loyola's greatest legacy is arguably the slim volume titled *The Spiritual Exercises*. This book is the centerpiece of Ignatian spirituality, and the *Exercises* lie at the foundation of the Society of Jesus. When the Jesuits adopted theater as an educational tool, the *Exercises* exerted a clear influence on the comedies and dramas written by Jesuits, for Jesuit students. In *Stratocles*, we see a number of passages where unmistakably Jesuit attitudes shine through.

The *Spiritual Exercises* are chiefly concerned with the discernment of spirits, and more specifically with opening one's self to good "motions of the soul" and rejecting the bad motions. This means that the Examen, or the series of guided prayers of self-examination found in the *Exercises*, is a teaching tool, a way to train the soul to follow the path God has set for an individual. Jesuit drama dutifully stresses the same message: characters like Stratocles who (eventually) fall in line with a Catholic ethic are the ones who succeed. Those who ignore the advice of their elders, who ignore the positive and negative motions of the soul, suffer great downfalls, like the title character in Jacob Bidermann's *Cenodoxus* (1602), a Dr. Faustus figure in perhaps the most widely admired and performed Jesuit Latin drama.[5] In

5. It was performed at Loyola College in Maryland in 1940; for an image of that production see http://contentdm.lndlibrary.org/cdm4/item_viewer.php?CISOROOT=/wrapper&CISOPTR=19&REC=1

many respects, *Stratocles* plays out like the proper discernment process, with a few missteps along the way.

The first and perhaps most essential requirement of participating in the exercises is imagination – something profoundly powerful within Ignatius himself, leading to his intense experience of conversion. That such powers of imagination would be drawn to drama is unsurprising. Theater is a powerful and flexible art form which can create, destroy, and rebuild reality on stage. In theater, actors and audience set disbelief aside and engage with characters that can range from the highly complex to the two-dimensional. In similar fashion, the imagination called for in the meditations of the *Exercises* asks an individual to conjure "synagogues, villages, and castles through which Christ our Lord passed as he preached" (§91).[6] For example, in the fifth contemplation of the second week, we also see "An Application of the Five Senses." The Jesuit mind is called "by the sight of my imagination...[to] see persons...listen to what they are saying...smell the fragrance and taste the infinite sweetness and charm of the Divinity...[and] using the sense of touch...embrace and kiss the places where the persons walk or sit" (§122-125). Even the minutest detail which the human mind can conjure is, in the *Spiritual Exercises*, meant to be dwelt upon so that we "will draw some profit from this" (§125).

Likewise, in Jesuit dramas we find detailed lists of feasts, elaborate sets, even casts of hundreds marshaled to accurately portray the clashes of kings and armies. Good theater demanded nothing less than the physical realization of whatever the imagination could conjure. In this play, the teacher Eubulus's hortatory monologues go into great detail about the evils which could visit a soldier, listing everything from an amputated ear to a cheating wife (190-219). Stratocles is the most imaginative of the characters, with his monologue at the end of Act I displaying a wealth of sensory imagery, from the pleasures of wine to the raw violence of stabbing an enemy soldier. Pontanus even uses spiritual vocabulary, employing the verb *meditari* (390) that

6 Ignatius 1991, 114-214.

connotes the "*meditatio*" as found in the first exercise (§45): Stratocles' fantasies of all the gory adventure and glory war can provide him appear to be a parody of contemplation or meditation in the Jesuit style.

In this sense, Stratocles becomes a prime example of the temptation which the *Exercises* warn against: "the enemy ordinarily proposes […] apparent pleasures" (§314). Stratocles seeks the glory and pride which the battlefield can give, as he tells Eubulus "you will look upon (eventually) [me as] a conqueror of many races, decorated with splendid spoils" (354-356). Pleasure is what drives this foolish student's decisions; he imagines that in winter quarters the soldier can "dine more lavishly and drink wine from bigger goblets and stay in bed peacefully clear into the middle of the day" (A1.10-A1.20).

Another echo of the *Examen's* ideas about temptation can be seen in Faustina in the last scene of the *Stratocles*, which illustrates sin and reconciliation as a battle between spiritual and physical strength. The *Exercises* describe temptation as a woman who "is weak against physical strength" and yet, in the face of weakness, her "anger, vindictiveness, and ferocity swell almost without limit" (§325). Faustina's wrath, when directed at her husband Misomachus, is nothing less than that of the "fourth fury" (A4.70). The conflict between Faustina and Misomachus even comes to blows: Misomachus must physically restrain Faustina (this stage business could be anything from a headlock to a desperate hold on her ankle). As the *Exercises* predict, it is only after Faustina is confronted by his threats and seems to be softened by them that a reconciliation ensues.

Though Stratocles strays toward the bad inclination of his soul, sources of reason emerge: the "good" spirits to whom Stratocles should listen. The first of these is his teacher, Eubulus. The professor, in vain, tries to impress the value of true discernment upon Stratocles: "There are three things which ought to be considered at length…chief among them, to enlist in the military" (153-155). Nevertheless, Stratocles, believing himself truly wise (but in fact merely stubborn), does not listen.

Eubulus then observes that "the young are led astray from the good by twin things: imprudence and their own strength" (291-292).

The tension between Stratocles and Eubulus stands as an allegory for the *Exercises'* emphasis on obedience. Ignatius boldly declares that "what I see as white, I will believe to be black if the hierarchical Church thus determines it" (§365). On a basic level, Stratocles the disobedient student is an example of how foolish it is not to follow one's elder, but the text goes into greater depth on authority. One section of dialogue between Eubulus and Stratocles discusses which authority to obey. Stratocles declares: "But is there any man who can live without laws? Who is subject to absolutely no one's authority? I would rather a man of decisive action command me..." (247-250). Stratocles is, perhaps, imagining the ideal human king described in the *Exercises*, who seeks "to conquer the whole land of infidels" (§93). Eubulus counters with parental authority, asking, "What then will your aged father say? What about your devoted mother, for whom you are the one and only?" (270-271).

Eventually, it takes the testimony of the returned soldiers, Misomachus and Tremonius, to convince Stratocles of the true nature of war – and of the generals under whom Stratocles would serve. "Whatever glory is taken from the conquered enemies in war becomes the commander's possession, not the soldier's" (505-507). The eyewitness testimony echoes the *Exercises*, as does the rhetorical argumentation in Tremonius's "But let this be the first point" (496), which sounds like the instructions of the Examen (§92-94). This information eventually prompts a conversion in Stratocles: "I am the one who was blind, but now I see most clearly" (545). Stratocles then becomes the voice of reason for Polemius, encouraging him to "follow me as I return to the straight and narrow" (580). In the end, when Stratocles comes around to the "straight and narrow," it is Eubulus's words he is reminded of, and the wisdom of his teacher's authority that prevails.

Stratocles serves as an example to students everywhere,

showing them where their true priorities should lie. A good Jesuit student must be thoughtful and discerning. He must avoid temptation. He must listen to his elders. Above all, he must realize the value of the education, intellectual and spiritual, that a Jesuit university can offer.

Konvitt in Dillingen 1627. Stich von Manasser.

Schoolyard of the Jesuit School in Dillingen (1627).

Just War and the Morality of Military Service

Stratocles' teacher Eubulus, in the midst of his attempt to dissuade his student from going off to fight, acknowledges the existence of a debate about whether and under what circumstances war was justified. "Would you say to me, 'Do you therefore wish that war never be waged? Do you wish that we bare our throats defenselessly to the enemy?' I want nothing of the sort. There is a time when waging war is useful, and indeed necessary ..." (219-223). The arguments for and against war that both student and teacher advance have their background in intellectual and theological debates in the sixteenth century and earlier that Pontanus will have known and exploited. The play can be seen as providing instruction in philosophy and theology as well as in Latin and rhetoric.

The seeds of the concept of a "just war" were sown by St. Augustine of Hippo in a letter written to Boniface, Count of Africa, in 418 A.D. In it, Augustine wrote "You must will to have peace, and be compelled by necessity to wage war, in order that God may free us from the necessity and preserve us in peace. We don't seek peace in order to incite war but we wage war in order to obtain peace. Be a peacemaker even when you are waging war, so that by overcoming those who attack you can beat them to the advantages of peace."[1] Thomas Aquinas further elaborated

1. Augustine. *Letter* 189, quoted from Augustine. *Letters*, trans. Leinenweber, p. 211. *Cf.* Augustine, *City of God*, I ch. 26, on God's supreme justification; IV ch. 4 and 6, on war as robbery; XV ch. 4, on the causes of war in the Earthly City; Augustine, *Letter* 138, to Marcellinus, particularly § 15.

this concept in his *Summa theologiae*. He declares that it is not always sinful to wage war, and that a war can be considered just if (1) a prince gives authorization, (2) it serves a just cause, (3) the intention is rightful.[2] Just wars are typically defensive in nature and are a response to some previous wrong. Therefore, the cause must be just in that it is avenging certain wrong actions that have been performed against a people, regaining something that was wrongfully seized, or if the offending nation is unwilling to make amends for some offensive action against the aggrieved nation. Right intention means that the purpose of the war is a just one, which is the advancement of good or the avoidance of evil. Proper authority means that a correct and legitimate authority for a principality, state, or nation is the only one who can declare this war. These requirements are commonly called *jus ad bellum*, or the justice/right to war. Related to these issues is the argument of proportionality, which mostly concerns actions in war and commands that no more intentional harm is done to one side than the other, especially not by the side that claims it is engaging in a just war. Obviously, both sides cannot claim to be fighting a just war unless one side is mistaken or a failure in initial diplomacy made the cause of the war uncertain. Therefore, it is expected that those who have proven they are engaging in a just war must remain just while the war is in progress, in accordance with *jus in bello* or justice/right in war.

During the sixteenth century, there were two prominent just war theorists in the Catholic Church: the Dominican friar Francisco de Vitoria (1483-1546) and Jesuit Francisco Suárez (1548-1617). Both Vitoria and Suárez expanded on St. Thomas' justification of war under certain circumstances, and each used Biblical support as well as Catholic social thought for his arguments. They agree that war is acceptable and sometimes even an aggressive war is necessary, "for the right of self-defense is natural and necessary."[3] Vitoria, however, also cautioned that while self-defense is perfectly understandable, it should be

2. Summa theologiae II-II 40 c.
3. Suárez, Disp. XIII: *On War*, section 1, nr. 5, p. 803 (ed. Williams and Davis) *On Charity*, disp. 13, pp. 800-865.

undertaken with "the minimum possible harm to the attacker," and that "if by resisting [a soldier] will be forced either to kill or gravely wound his attacker, it seems that he is required to take any possible opportunity of escape by running away."[4] An important question in the political climate of the 16th century was whether princes who are Christians are particularly justified in fighting wars against nonbelievers.[5]

The Jesuit Franciscus Toletus (1532-1596), who commented on Thomas' *Summa*, identified three heretical positions: (1) every war is a mortal sin (allegedly the opinion of the Manicheans and Erasmus); (2) wars in the Old Testament could be justified through the "Old Law", but since the advent of Christ it is not legal to wage war (a position held by Johannes Oecolampadius, who died in 1531 and was one of the Protestant reformers); (3) even though some wars are justified, the war against the Turks was not, for Luther maintained that God had sent the Turks as a punishment for the Christians.[6] Toletus referred back, among others, to Augustine, who in his *Reply to Faustus* (book 22) refuted allegations issued by Faustus, a member of the Manichean sect. The Manichaeans believed in an evil deity that counteracted God and taught that Moses acted immorally when he waged war (chapter 5). From chapter 69 on, Augustine justified Moses' actions as prompted by zeal and divine command. Here Augustine also listed criteria for justified war. This text by Augustine was probably the source for Toletus's accusation: when he discussed the first heresy listed above, he thought that in opposing war Erasmus was siding with Manichean heresy. However, Erasmus distanced himself from Martin Luther's strict refusal of any military resistance against the Turks.[7]

In Pontanus' play the almost reluctant remark about the necessity of war and Stratocles' resolve to fight in Hungary against the Turks can be read, and was certainly perceived in the audience, against this theoretical backdrop.

4. Vitoria, *On the Law of War* I.2.1, p. 299. (ed. Padgen and Lawrence)
5. Suárez, *On War,* section 5.
6. Toletus, *In Summam Theologiae S. Thomae Aquinatis Enarratio*, vol. 2, Quaestio 34, art. 1, p. 225.
7. Erasmus, *On the Turkish War* (Collected Works, volume 64), p. 234, note 134.

The Morality of Soldiers

The debate about the justification for war, harkening back to Aquinas and Augustine, was not the only important question. Fiercely contested was also the issue of how military service affects the morality of individuals. Thomas de Vio Cajetan, O.P., (1489-1534) had declared in his handbook for confessors that the individual soldier does not have to question the justification of the war while he is enlisted in an army. However, it was considered sinful to join the battle only to get plunder.[8] Toletus emphasized that from the right intention and the proportionality of warfare it follows that not only military leaders but also ordinary soldiers are involved in the morality of waging war. He mentioned expressly that there exist secondary intentions or moral dangers that run contrary to just war, such as looting and revenge. Therefore, if military leaders wage a war with wrong intentions, they encourage common soldiers to behave immorally.[9] He concluded, reiterating Cajetan's view, that (1) a soldier is not allowed to participate in a battle if its cause is dubious; that (2) soldiers who are in doubt about the justification of the war do not commit a sin while serving under a commander if they had enrolled in a time of peace; that (3) soldiers who are not bound to any command may not join a war while in doubt about its justification.[10]

Suárez also addressed the question of the morality of soldiers. He concluded that mercenaries, since they are a sub-category of the larger classification "soldiers", do not have to question the justification of a war as long as there is no concrete reason to do so; and even if there are reasons for doubt, mercenaries are still "bound to follow the course of action which is more probably just" in case they cannot ascertain the truth of the matter. In this way, using an argument of so-called probabilism, Suárez laid the ethical burden of justification on the shoulders of the Prince or military leader.[11] A commonplace used in this context was the

8. Cajetan, *Summula*, pp. 25-30; specifically p. 29.
9. Toletus, Quaestio 34, art. 1, dubium 1, pp. 227-228.
10. Toletus, Quaestio 34, art. 1, dubium 4, p. 229.
11. Suárez, sect. 6, nr. 12, p. 836.

advice John the Baptist gave to the soldiers: "Do violence to no man, neither accuse any falsely; and be content with your wages." (Luke 3:14) This could be read as a condemnation of warfare, but also as a confirmation of the soldiers' submission to their leaders.

Antonio Possevino, S.J., (1533-1611) a diplomat and bibliographer, discussed the military in his annotated bibliography, *Bibliotheca Selecta*, where he drafted a potential manual for soldiers and their priests who are in military service, which offers a wealth of information on the vast amount of late medieval and Renaissance books on the topic.[12] In his own book *The Christian Soldier* (*Il Soldato Christiano*), about the desired virtues of soldiers and officers in the war against the heretics and heathens of his time,[13] Possevino presents a practical guide to honest behavior in war, including the dangers of being captured by the enemy. First and foremost, however, he stressed the maintenance of Christian piety in spite of the temptations of military life. This was certainly designed as an answer to Erasmus and other 16th-century opponents of war. At the same time, Possevino reinterpreted the metaphor of Christian life as **militia** or military service that had been employed most recently by Erasmus of Rotterdam in his *Handbook for the Christian Soldier* (*Enchiridion Militis Christiani*), a metaphor dear to Christianity since St. Paul's *Epistle to the Ephesians* (6:10-20).[14] An otherwise unknown Hieronymus Spartanus (perhaps the Humanist Eobanus Hessus, 1488-1540) wrote in 1540 a poem *Miles Christianus* that was intended to be a commentary on *Ephesians*.[15] It opened with remarks that resonate in Stratocles's attitude: "Dulcis inexpertis equidem Mars esse videtur / Ociam militiam turba cruenta putat" (Mars seems sweet to those who don't know him, and the bloodthirsty crowd finds military service entertaining.) The comparison between life and strife was to be taken literally in the sixteenth century, when the Christians

12. Possevinus, *Bibliotheca selecta* book 5, chapters 6-8.
13. Possevino, *Il Soldato Christiano* , entire.
14. See Harnack; also Wang, esp. on Erasmus pp. 158-163.
15. Printed in Basel: Oporinus 1550 (http://www.uni-mannheim.de/mateo/camena/spartanus1/te01.html).

believed themselves to be endangered by the Turkish army and were forced to defend the faith in military actions, if necessary. The same overlapping of metaphorical and practical meaning of **militia** could already be found in the Dominican St. Antonine of Florence (1389-1459), who had interpreted the war between nations as an intensified version of human contention. Therefore he treated war under the heading of homicide.[16]

All those theoretical considerations are reflected in the discussions of Pontanus' play, specifically in Act I, the exchange between Eubulus and Stratocles on the horrors and honors of military life. In another play, which was produced at the Jesuit school of Ingolstadt in 1606, an allegory warned against joining the military: "A reckless and inexperienced soldier wants to go to Hungary and to fight there for several years. He equips himself with weaponry. He is approached by Time who announces his death. But the young and strong man doesn't want to hear about dying but, rather, challenges Death. When he turns to him and sees him he drops his rifle and gets shot by Death, who praises the rifle as a very convenient tool for killing people."[17] In 1580 Pontanus had a student discuss the scholarly question: "What Is More Important in War: Virtue or Fortune?" The answer was that in war virtue and fortune are both necessary. Although fortune was interpreted as divine support, the disputation illustrated its arguments with examples from ancient battles and rituals in the humanist vein.[18]

Ethical concerns acquired a higher level of urgency during the Thirty Years War, when mercenaries were very frequently underpaid, starving, and got no share of the spoils.[19] Therefore Rodrigo de Arriaga (1592-1667), the most significant Jesuit theologian after Suárez, complained in the middle of his treatise on just war: "Good Lord! What do we see these days with our eyes, how many captains … increase the number of soldiers in

16. Antoninus, *Summae Sacrae Theologiae*, part 3, titulus 4, cap. 1-2, fol. 63r-69v.
17. Summary translated from [Anonymous] *Von dem Todt oder Todtentantz*, reprinted in Szarota 1980, vol. II 2, p. 2034.
18. Leinsle, *Disputationes* 2006, 485 and note 91; the Latin title of the thesis was *Valeatne plus in bellis virtus an Fortuna?*
19. Duhr, vol. II 2 (1913), 471.

order to have more stipends, which they keep to themselves? ... It is a miracle that God is not so disturbed by this kind of military that he destroys the whole world."[20]

20. Arriaga, disp. 28, sect. 3, subsect. 1, n. 42, p. 624.

College and church of St. Salvator in Augsburg (1679).

A Play about War and the Real Wars in Pontanus' Time

The play makes frequent reference to contemporary political and military conflicts, and this provides insight into the context that spawned the work. These references change in the various versions of the play that we possess; this illustrates both the evolution of the text and the quickly changing religious and political climate in which Pontanus lived and the play was performed.

Various versions of *Stratocles*,[1] published or copied at different times, mention an assortment of contemporary political and religious conflicts (see lines 369-70 and 552 with our notes). Stratocles, the eager would-be soldier, declares himself ready to join different conflicts in the various versions of the play that are extant. In the oldest manuscript (1578), Stratocles says he intends to join Don Juan de Austria in putting down the revolt of the Netherlands. In the second manuscript (1580), Stratocles is rushing off to join Don Juan de Austria's successor, Alessandro Farnese, who has taken over as the governor of the Netherlands. At that time, Farnese was continuing the campaign against the rebels in the Northern Provinces of the Netherlands and turned his attention to the French war of religion between the Huguenots and Catholics. In the printed edition of 1594, Stratocles is off to support the Holy (Catholic)

1. On the various versions of the *Stratocles* see Rädle 1979, 556-559 and 595, which gives his list of variants for lines 369-70, where the different versions appear; Leinsle 2005, 133-135; see our introduction, section on history of the text.

League to rout the Huguenots from France and save the throne from the Huguenot, Henry Prince of Navarre. Lastly, in the printed edition of *Stratocles* in 1600, Stratocles leaves to wage war against the Ottoman Empire which has threatened Europe throughout the 16th Century but is beginning slowly to decline in power. Examining the references to wars within the various versions of the play *Stratocles* provides a glimpse of the religious as well as political conflicts in Europe during the 16th century.

In the oldest extant version of *Stratocles*, Stratocles declares he is departing to join Don Juan de Austria in the Netherlands. Don Juan de Austria became famous across Europe for his military success before he took up his post as Governor of the Netherlands in 1576. Born the illegitimate son of Emperor Charles V Habsburg of the Holy Roman Empire and the half brother of King Philip II Habsburg of Spain, he was kept secluded in Spain in his early life. After the death of his father, Don Juan was recognized by Philip II as his half brother and given the name Don Juan de Austria. He joined the Spanish military in his youth and on October 5, 1571 led the Holy Alliance of Spain, Venice and the Holy See to victory in the Battle of Lepanto against the Ottoman Empire.

After the battle Don Juan was left in limbo for a while before Philip II appointed him Governor General of the Netherlands in 1576. The Netherlands had been in a state of rebellion since 1572 when William the Silent of Orange (a Protestant aristocrat) unified the Northern Provinces. Don Juan arrived and brought about the signing of the Perpetual Edict, which had the rebellious regions recognize Don Juan as governor of the Netherlands and restore Catholicism as the official religion within the region. Holland and Zeeland, however, refused to sign the treaty, and Don Juan returned to campaigning. He died in October of 1578, leaving his successor Alessandro Farnese, the Duke of Parma, in charge of the pacification of the Netherlands.[2]

In the second manuscript, Stratocles abandons his studies

2. See Geyl 150-169 for more detail.

to join the Duke of Parma in his pacification of the Northern Provinces. Farnese was well known for his military genius and diplomacy, able to persuade enemy agents to defect and to drive those who did not into submission. He was also well known for his use of mercenary troops in battle, among which Stratocles would have fought had he reached the front. Farnese came close to recapturing all of the Netherlands, but Queen Elizabeth I of England intervened in 1586, sending reinforcements and supplies to aid the people of the Northern Provinces. This act led to the attempted Spanish invasion of England, but the Spanish Armada failed twice, which damaged Spain's finances as well as its international reputation. After these defeats Spain's position in the Netherlands worsened. Nonetheless, Farnese was instructed in 1590 to relieve the Siege of Paris and ordered back into France both in 1591 and in 1592 to assist with the Huguenot conflict. While doing his duty for Spain in France in 1592 he fell ill and died in Arras.[3]

In the 1594 printed edition of the play, Stratocles leaves to join the Catholic forces fighting against the Huguenots of France in the French religious civil war. The decisive war of religion in France was the War of the Three Henrys, 1587-1589, between Henry III Valois King of France, Henry I of Lorraine, The Duke of Guise and Henry Bourbon Prince of Navarre. Religious fighting had continued intermittently in France since 1562 with stretches of both open warfare and unsteady peace.[4] These periods of quiet and conflict continued until August of 1572 when a marriage treaty was struck between Henry Prince of Navarre and Margaret Valois, the sister of King Henry III and King Charles IX. This treaty did not hold up, because on August 24, 1572 the current French King Charles IX, under the influence of his council and the League, massacred the Huguenot leaders in Paris and sparked a slaughter of Huguenots all over France, which came to be known as the St. Bartholomew's Day Massacre.[5] By abjuring his faith Henry Prince of Navarre

3. See Cummins 717-721 for a fuller account.
4. Coffin and Stacy 502-504.
5. Knecht 42-51.

barely escaped death and was held captive in court for many months until his escape.[6] Charles IX died in 1574 and Henry III Valois was crowned in 1575. Upon the death of Henry III's last brother, François Valios Duke d'Anjou, Navarre became the heir apparent to the throne of France. In 1585, the Treaty of Nemours was signed by the League and Henry III of France, excluding Navarre from succession. In 1587, Navarre's and Henry III's army met at Coutras where Henry III's army was defeated. The League in the same year also had a victory in which it drove back the German Protestants who were coming to the aid of the French Huguenots. Guise defeated the Germans both at Vimory and Auneau and marched his victorious army into Paris, a popular stronghold of the League, forcing Henry III to flee Paris. Guise, with the League, forced Henry III to sign the Edict of Union in 1588 that named Guise the Lieutenant General of France. Henry III struck back at this challenge to the throne and on October 23, 1588 had Guise and his brother assassinated. The League continued to control Paris, which brought about reconciliation between Henry III and Navarre. This reconciliation led to their march on and joint siege of Paris on July 30, 1588. Two days later Henry III of France was stabbed to death in his headquarters, leaving Navarre heir to the throne, which he assumed as Henry IV. Nonetheless, it was not until 1598 that the Peace of Vervins and the Edict of Nantes finally brought the wars of religion to an end in France.[7]

The above sketches cover the references to European conflicts. The latest versions of the play call attention to foreign invaders: The Ottomans. The Ottoman Empire during the late 16th and early 17th centuries was no longer viewed as unconquerable, as it had been earlier. In the middle of the 16th century Europeans widely feared them,[8] and the Vatican also in 1551 hastily raised an army out of fear that the Turks were on their way to Rome.[9] On October 7, 1571, however, the

6. Thompson 450, 514.
7. Knecht 65-83.
8. Cf. Setton 536, "the Venetians lived in perennial fear of the Turks."
9. Setton 539.

Ottomans were defeated at the battle of Lepanto. The battle is known for having raised European morale by having "obviously shown that the Turks were not invincible."[10] If not decisive, the battle nonetheless appears quickly to have brought about change: after Lepanto, the Ottomans signed peace treaties with both Venice and Spain, bringing some of the major conflicts between European powers and the Ottomans to an end. The Austrians, on the other hand, chose a different path by beginning a war in the Balkans that lasted from 1593 until 1606. In the play's 1600 printed version it is to this war that Stratocles and Polemius are headed. Stratocles' statement that he will kill "thousands of Turks" (370) perhaps reflects the belief that the Turks were no longer invincible and also possibly betrays a belief in the decline of the Ottoman Empire. The reference is topical and may betray some contemporary attitudes. Chiefly, however, it demonstrates his naiveté about war, as is the case throughout the play.

10. Setton 1099.

The Characters and Their Names

There are six characters in *Stratocles or War*, each offering an individual perspective on the play's central themes of education and war. The characters' roles are summarized by their Latinized Greek or Latin names, which serve also to illuminate some of Pontanus' thoughts on various issues treated in the play.

Stratocles, the main character, is presented as a glory-seeking, naïve young man. Strato, from the Greek **stratos** meaning army, and –kles from **kleos**, the Greek word for glory, combine to form the name Stratocles. Literally translated this would mean something like "Martial Glory"; a more colloquial and free translation would be "Captain Gung-ho". The name thus reveals the young student's personality.

Especially toward the beginning of the play we see this "speaking name" illustrated, as young Stratocles voices a desire to rescue the hope for glory he fears is dying in his idle life as a student; he claims to prefer the supposed riches of battle. The play opens with a diatribe from Stratocles against school and scholarship, showing the sort of impatient attitude one might expect of a contemporary high school student interested in jettisoning his studies and striking out into a real-world adventure. Stratocles proceeds to imagine an alternative to all the monotony: becoming a soldier and fighting in a war.

Yet it quickly becomes evident that Stratocles is no more fit for war than a child, for his renunciation of school and glorification of battle are revealed as a combination of misconception and naïve desire. Confronted with Eubulus' warnings against the life of a soldier, Stratocles displays sheer ignorance of barracks life as he champions the glory of killing and plundering foreign enemies, and reduces the more immediate turmoil of war (death, disease, harsh living conditions and strict orders) to his romantic conception of "the makings of manliness" (line 254).

Stratocles' eagerness for battle is countered by the arguments of our second character, Eubulus the teacher, whose words become the wisdom of the play. Indeed, Eubulus' name translates as something like "Wise Counselor" from the Greek **eu-**, good or well, and **boule**, meaning counsel, plan or advice.

Eubulus warns Stratocles in so many words that he has no idea what war has in store for a young man, that battle should be avoided, and that Stratocles will surely face disappointment and incomprehensible suffering if he pursues his course toward combat. It is evident through his words not only that Eubulus cares about Stratocles' well-being, but also that the teacher is aware of his student's intelligence and scholarly aptitude (qualities that are not, however, consistently on view in the course of the play). These traits, declares Eubulus, when present in cultured youth, are not meant to be wasted in battle. Stratocles is, of course, resistant to this notion. He wants to break free from the bondage of student life and learn about the world's riches himself.

It is no surprise, then, that Eubulus' appeal to the good life of scholarship and to the pursuit of wisdom falls on deaf ears in Stratocles, for the young man is full of the hubris of youth and longs for the pleasures of life (e.g., the women and drink alluded to in Stratocles' address after verse 389, lines A1.1-24). Eubulus is of course aware that Stratocles is plagued by the capriciousness of youth and is blinded by ambition, but he tries nonetheless to steer his student away from imminent danger.

The contrasts between Stratocles and Eubulus are revealed most poignantly when Stratocles presents himself to his teacher wearing battle-gear. Eubulus says that the young man's appearance has "never been more repulsive" (line 344), but Stratocles is preoccupied with what amounts to playing soldier. Eubulus is resigned to the futility of his cautions and fears for Stratocles, yet he is somewhat confident that his pupil's intellect will come into play sooner or later and eventually lead Stratocles to recognize the brutality of war and return to his studies. Their parting words illustrate this fact and leave the primary conflict of the play to be resolved by further interaction.

The next characters on the scene are Tremonius and Misomachus, ex-soldiers and acquaintances of Stratocles returning home from war. Their names reveal what could be a sarcastic joke employed by Pontanus. Tremonius comes from **tremor**, or **tremere**, to fear, or, possibly, **tre-** and **mon-**, meaning "thrice warned". Although we discover Tremonius' beneficent role in helping to deter Stratocles from going to war, he could be named here as "Mr. Chickenheart". Of course, the name could also be intended to have a more direct meaning that reflects the genuine existential fear of death and suffering that is a major component of a soldier's reality, and that Tremonius is supposed to help convey to the young Stratocles. In this case, the extreme fear denoted by Tremonius' name may be regarded in fact as a positive attribute.

Likewise for Misomachus: his name could be translated as "Battle-hater" or "Scaredy-cat". Miso, from **misos** or **miseo**, to hate, and machos from **mache** or **machomai**, meaning battle or fight, contribute to this other "speaking" name. Again, the name Misomachus could also be intended to have a more straightforward and salutary significance. "Battle-hater" could be regarded as a title reflecting the ex-soldier's rather wise conversion from warrior to deserter.

The dualism of the returning soldiers' names may reflect the fact that they are initially viewed by Stratocles and his companion as lowly cowards, as the sarcastic, mocking version of their names suggests; and then after conversation with the boys, they are viewed more favorably as prophets of truth, suggesting the more positive connotations latent in their "speaking" names. The two battered soldiers do indeed echo some of Eubulus' cautions about war, and they exhibit the filth and injury foretold by the wise teacher. They offer Stratocles a view of what he might look like after combat, and present some living proof of Eubulus' predictions to the student who is wise enough to heed them.

Tremonius and Misomachus are glad to be home and wish to convince their young acquaintances, Stratocles and Polemius (Stratocles' friend and fellow glory-seeker), that there is nothing, including being a fearless soldier, better than being alive. They argue that the role of the warrior risks the most precious gift: life on earth. The ex-soldiers speak of their departure for battle as a definite mistake, and moreover are thankful to have survived such stupidity. This too links their experience with the words of Eubulus.

Polemius is adamant in his initial rejection of the perceived weakness of Tremonius and Misomachus. This illustrates the correlation between his function in the play and the meaning of his name, which can be translated roughly as "Warmonger". It derives from **polemos**, meaning war, and the adjective ending of Polem**ius**' name meaning "having to do with". Polemius exhibits a rather dim-witted drive for a harsh reality he knows nothing about, a conviction presumably formed from entreaties for battle voiced by his friend Stratocles. The accounts of the returning soldiers, based on harsh experience, serve only to strengthen Polemius' passion for war, and the reader wonders whether or not Polemius even understands or agrees with Stratocles' ultimate decision to turn back from battle. He seems simply to follow Stratocles and to suffer more than a slight amount of hesitation or confusion at his friend's change of mind. This suggests that Polemius might well be highly malleable, a fierce proponent of anything presented to him with adequate persuasion (especially from Stratocles).

All the brashness of Stratocles is sufficiently countered by the dual effect of his teacher's words and the corroborating testimonials of Tremonius and Misomachus, thus confirming

Eubulus' frequent mention of his student's latent intelligence. Further proof of the wisdom behind Eubulus' condemnation of war appears in the following sections that feature Faustina and her conflict with her returning husband, Misomachus.

Faustina is a wife abandoned through the same blind desire that threatens to relieve Stratocles of his fortunate position in life and, in Eubulus' words, is likely to leave Stratocles' parents childless before they die. She is distraught after years of barely supporting her family by lowly means, and claims she is willing to appear a "Lioness or Tigress" (A3.59) to her no-good husband upon his return (if he returns). When Misomachus *does* arrive home, she is understandably irate and has no trouble eloquently denouncing the injustice that has been done to her by her husband (and by war). Hence, her name Faustina, meaning something like "Fistful of Fortune", derived from Faust, meaning fist, and **–ina**, a dimunitive; so in German, "little fist". Also, **faust-** means blessed, fortunate or smiled upon by gods or fate in Latin, so along with indicating the angry reception she gives her husband, Faustina's name is an ironic title that emphasizes the rather *un*fortunate existence of a wife left destitute and deprived by war. Indeed, Faustina's monologues and treatment of Misomachus act as humorous denunciations of the domestic consequences of war, and therefore contribute to the overall anti-war theme of the play.

In Pontanus' comedy, the characters are aided by their names in offering commentary on the central themes. The folly of war is underscored, as well as the wisdom and truth available through education. Through the humorous and creative use of the characters' names, Pontanus is able to put forward a dramatically pleasing version of his vision of Jesuit education.

Titelblatt von Pontans Kommentar zu Virgil 1599.

Title page of Pontanus' commentary on Virgil (1599).

Pontanus' Use of Classical Sources

Pontanus was a deeply learned man and especially expert in Latin and Greek. He was professor in charge of instruction in those languages at various schools, and adept at creation of literature in Latin across a range of genres (e.g. oratory, elegy and other types of poetry, and, of course, drama).[1] Like the humanists of his day,[2] he was steeped in Classical literature and committed to securing its place in the curriculum of Jesuit schools (see Appendix on Humanistic Studies). His thorough familiarity with Classical literature is on display in *Stratocles*: quotations, adaptations and allusions to authors both famous and obscure appear on every page.

The notes at the end of the translation examine these references individually. Rädle in his notes discussed the most obvious allusions. We have been able to confirm or correct him where he has posited a literary reference by using modern information technology that was unavailable to him in his 1979 edition. We were also able to expand significantly his list of allusions to include many isolated verbal reminiscences or quotations, sometimes just a single odd or rarely encountered form. In most cases we include in the notes a discussion of the likely or possible meaning of the allusion in context; i.e.,

1. See Leinsle 2006, *Dilinganae* 79-85, 481-485 for oratory, and 2005 and 2006 *Jahrbuch* for other genres.
2. On Jesuit humanism see Fumaroli 1975, and on Pontanus the humanist see especially Bauer.

what would have been the probable import of a reference to a Classical author for Pontanus' composite audience, comprised of both schoolboys at one level and erudite humanists at another. We have probably missed some that would have been detected by others as learned as Pontanus.

Jesuit school drama was openly didactic, and one of its aims was familiarizing students with proper usage and good style in Latin.[3] It is thus not surprising that Pontanus peppers his text with frequent references to authors from antiquity who were revered for their literary skill, power and elegance. The writers who figured most prominently in the standard Latin curriculum, Vergil and Cicero, are together those most often quoted or referenced (25 clear or probable allusions). *Stratocles* is a comedy, so it makes sense that the author most frequently alluded to is Plautus (17 times), a prolific master of Roman comic verse and an author especially beloved by Pontanus. In contrast, Pontanus makes only two references to Terence, the other exemplar of Roman comedy and praised in the Renaissance and after for his pure diction and style. Among Greek authors Homer is most often alluded to (6 times), and Aristotle is specifically invoked twice (disparagingly) in discussions of the curriculum put in the mouths of students. Other poets repeatedly referenced are Ovid (11), Catullus (5) and Horace (4). Perhaps unsurprisingly in a work in verse, poets receive allusions far more often than prose authors.

In all, according to our reckoning, Pontanus in these roughly 800 lines makes reference to 27 Latin authors from antiquity and 4 Greek authors. These allusions range from the standard authorities discussed above to single references to very obscure writers like Baebius Italicus, or to those that exist in mere fragments, like Ennius. In Greek he alludes to Aristotle, Hesiod, Homer and Plutarch. In Latin those referenced, either securely or possibly, are Augustine, Baebius Italicus, Caesar, Catullus, Cicero, the *Disticha Catonis* (a collection that includes both early and post-Classical material), Ennius, Horace, Isidore

3. See especially Bielmann 1982.

of Seville, Juvenal, Livy, Lucan, Lucretius, Martial, Ovid (the *Art of Love, Fasti* and *Letters* in addition to the *Metamorphoses*), Persius, Plautus (more often than any other single author), Pliny the Younger, Sallust, Seneca, Servius, Silius Italicus, Terence, Vegetius and Vergil.

Among post-Classical but "classicizing" authors by far the most frequently alluded to or quoted is Erasmus (13 clear or probable references). *Stratocles* is deeply indebted to some of Erasmus' essays on war, chiefly the *Complaint of Peace* and *Dialogue of a Soldier and a Carthusian* (see section on Just War), so quotations or adaptations of those essays are unsurprising. Moreover, Pontanus and other Jesuit educators were fond of using proverbs as a way of teaching Latin. We thus encounter six references to Erasmus' collection of aphorisms, his *Adages*.

The picture that emerges from this wide and tightly interwoven web of allusions is one consistent with what we gather from Pontanus' own writings and biography: a man of both wide and deep learning, sensitive to literary texture from the level of the individual word to the overarching tone of an entire work. *Stratocles* is a didactic work pitched to a specific audience at a specific time, but its deep literary roots, watered by the erudition of its author, spread in many directions and allow it to speak to audiences far removed in space and time.

Beginning of *Stratocles* in the manuscript M2 (see p. 53);
courtesy of Ulrich G. Leinsle, Regensburg

The History of the Text of "Stratocles"

We possess six versions of *Stratocles, sive Bellum*, and the differences between them range from the trivial to the significant. These incarnations are spread out between the years 1578 and 1600. Rädle (1979, pp. 556-559) and Leinsle (2005, esp. 133-135; 2006) give full descriptions of the manuscripts and printed editions that together comprise our witnesses to the various stages of the piece's composition. As we describe above (in the section How to Use this Book), two of these versions, discussed below, are of primary importance. In creating a sensible and readable edition, we, like Rädle before us, rely chiefly on the last printed version of 1600 ("B" in Rädle's conspectus, which we follow with some modifications; see below for more specifics). The other most important witness to the text is a manuscript we call "M5," which exists in only one version and includes material not found in the others. This manuscript includes additions made by Pontanus for a special performance of the play in 1590 on Mardi Gras, the Tuesday before Ash Wednesday. On that day moral strictures were relaxed and otherwise forbidden material could be presented, as we shall see. This version includes instructions as to where in the shorter version of the play the additions were to be inserted. Rädle printed these sections as various appendices to his 1979 critical edition. As we explain above, we decided to create a running text that includes these lines where they were to appear in the performance.

The information below is taken from the findings of Rädle and Leinsle and attempts to lay out the various sources in brief but clear compass.

I. Printed versions

A = the first printing of *Stratocles* that appeared in 1594 in Ingolstadt on pages 563-688 of the following book: *Jacobi Pontani de Societate Jesu Poeticarum institutionum libri tres. Eiusdem Tyrocinium poeticum. Ingolstadii, Ex Typographia Davidis Sartorii Anno MDXCIV* ("The Jesuit Jacobus Pontanus' *Three Books on the Rules for Poetry*; by the same author, *An Introduction to Poetry*. Ingolstadt, David Sartorius Press, 1594").[1] The *Introduction to Poetry* of this edition contains various types of poems and an Old Testament play on the sacrifice of Isaac in addition to the *Stratocles*. In 1597, a second corrected edition of the *Rules for Poetry* appeared, but it lacks the *Introduction to Poetry*, and hence the *Stratocles*.

B = the third edition of Pontanus' works that appeared in 1600: *Jacobi Pontani de Societate Jesu Poeticarum Institutionum libri III. Editio tertia cum auctario et Indice hactenus desiderato. Eiusdem Tyrocinium poeticum cum supplemento. Ingolstadii, Ex Typographia Adamis Sartorii Anno MDC.* The titles are the same as in A, but this edition contains various supplements (e.g., a new tragedy based on a bible story that did not appear in the earlier editions) and an index. The *Stratocles* is on pages 593-616.

II. Manuscripts[2]

M1 = a version not extant today, but one that clearly

---

1. See Rädle 1979, 557-8 for more details.
2. The manuscripts are listed, like the printed sources above, chronologically *according to the parts that contain* Stratocles. These documents were often put together over a period of years, and the manuscripts contain documents that begin and end at different times. Our listing here is based on the information available that allows us to list the versions of the play from oldest to youngest.

served as the source for most of our extant manuscripts. Scholars can compare errors and omissions in two or more manuscripts and determine whether they were copied from the same source. Rädle (1979, 556-557) found that two manuscripts described below (M3[3] and M5) depend on this same source, M1. M2 was unknown to Rädle, but Leinsle holds that M2 is also dependent on M1. However, in light of various differences between M2 and the group M3 and M5, he deems it an independent witness to M1. This means that M2 was not copied or corrected from the other later manuscripts M3 and M5, but stems from the earlier version, M1 (Leinsle 2005, 134-135).

M2 = Dillingen codex XV.399, produced between 1574 and 1585 (Leinsle 2005, 88). It contains many different texts, and the version of the play contained herein is the earliest that we have, as proven by the notation that it was performed in 1578 (**Dialogus Dillingae habitus anno** 1578). This early incarnation of the play was unknown to Rädle, who does not include it in his list of witnesses to the text. It appears to be related to M1. Leinsle (2005, esp. 88-97 and 133-135) gives a detailed description of the manuscript, its contents and history. This earliest version is a dialogue restricted to the two characters Stratocles and Eubulus (see section above on Characters). This is followed by two other pieces that share thematic affinities with the 1590 version of the play and were, like that version, presented on Mardi Gras (see Appendix on Renaissance Hazing).

Professor Leinsle graciously provided us with images of the relevant pages of this manuscript (folios 263 recto to 277 recto),[4] which we transcribed and compared to Rädle's

---

3. This is "H1," or "manuscript 1," in Rädle's 1979 edition. We have attempted to avoid the confusion likely to develop in comparing the different lists of manuscripts by listing things chronologically.

4. These are technical terms in paleography, or the study of manuscripts. A folio is a sheet of paper in a book, and the recto is the side one encounters first when reading (on the "right" (*recto*) side of the book), while the verso is on the other side when one "turns" (*verso*) the page.

text. It offers variants from the first act that are at times significant.[5] Most of the differences consist of adaptations of or references to material from Classical authors (primarily Vergil, Horace and Plautus) that are loosely related to the immediate context (most often, the nature of adolescent males) but not strictly relevant or necessary to the plot. In subsequent versions many of these lines were dropped. Other variations include references to contemporary events that changed with the different times of performance. See our section above on the wars referred to in the play for a discussion of the various contemporary military conflicts that are mentioned in the versions from 1578 to 1600. This manuscript also allowed us at one point to correct Rädle's text and translation (see our note at line 234).

M3 = Dillingen codex XV 223, folio 164 verso to 174 verso (Rädle's H1). This is by far the more accurate and legible of the two manuscripts that stem from M1. Jakob Gretser, another important German Jesuit dramatist, personally penned this manuscript, which contains primarily works by Pontanus and Gretser. It was assembled between the years 1580 and 1585.

M4 = another manuscript depending on M1 above, namely Vienna codex 9839, folio 46 recto to 54 verso. Michael Rubin, a student at Dillingen who graduated in 1582, produced this manuscript. This text is full of errors and does not offer any reliable help in constituting the text of the play. It does, however, supply important information about the performance history of the piece.

The title page of this manuscript indicates that it was begun in 1580, and the last piece in the collection is dated to June 1583. On folio 54, at the end of the *Stratocles*, is

---

5. Leinsle 2005, 134 note 143 gives a list of the most striking differences. Perhaps chief among them is the fact that Stratocles' expression of desire to leave school in order to enlist is missing, which makes the dialogue a much more "academic" exercise. The dramatic situation that we find in later versions of the play is far more compelling.

this entry: "put on successfully by Professor Pontanus in the school at Dillingen." We know from elsewhere that the play was "revived" successfully at Dillingen in 1590, but since the last entry of this manuscript is from 1583, and since there is no other sign of later correction, this entry is very unlikely to refer to the 1590 version. It seems then that the entry is making reference to the "premier" of the play sometime in 1580 in Dillingen, before Pontanus moved to Augsburg. Another entry in the chronicles of the college at Augsburg indicates a performance of the *Stratocles* there in 1588.

M5 = Dillingen codex XV 221, folio 194 recto to 208 recto, with an unnumbered leaf between 196 and 197. This manuscript contains a number of works (not all listed here) that give some idea of the literary range of Pontanus and some of his Jesuit colleagues: Pontanus' own edition of Plautus' *Captivi*, with additions in German, probably for productions in Dillingen in 1574 and 1588; a Christmas dialogue, a small play done in Dillingen in 1588; two pieces probably by the Jesuit dramatist Gretser (see above on M2), a comedy about Solomon and a dialogue on the sacrament of communion, with dates of their respective productions; a play by the English Jesuit Edmund Campion about Ambrosius of Milan; a play on the sacrifice of Isaac by Pontanus that was performed in 1591 in Dillingen; and the *Stratocles*, identified in this entry as a "dialogue" produced in Dillingen in 1590 on Mardi Gras: *Dialogus ad Bacchanalia qui Stratocles dicitur*.

This manuscript is of primary importance, for it is the only one that includes the parts with Faustina, a wife of one of the characters (see section above on characters). We also have some information about the success of this version, for in the chronicles of the University of Dillingen for 1590 we read the following: **in bacchanalibus actus dialogus Stratocles dataque convictoribus praemia,** "the play/dialogue *Stratocles* was performed on Mardi Gras and prizes were given to the winners."

The various versions of the play allow us to see Pontanus the poet, teacher and dramatist at work, generating pedagogical instruments that combined Classical material, references to contemporary events, and lines reflecting the realities of his students' daily lives. In his hands the drama juxtaposes the old and the new and attempts to make both strands alive, accessible and often funny. These versions reveal Pontanus the dramatist as always working as the teacher of rhetoric, trying to combine the **dulce**, what is pleasant, charming and attractive, with the **utile**, what is useful (both practically and morally). We believe that *Stratocles* succeeds in both areas.

Performance

This translation of *Stratocles* received its first performance by the Halfshire Players on 25 July, 2008 in Richland, NY at the Half-Shire Historical Society. Loyola student Erin Bacon played the title role and directed, and Loyola student Christian Klarner appeared as Misomachus.

I. BALDE. S. I.

IEPHTIAS.

TRAGOEDIA.

Titelblatt von Balde, Jephtias.
Stich von Wolfg. Kilian (¹/₁).

A soldier and a sutler on the title page of a Jesuit play by Jacobus Balde (1604-68).

Stratocles or War

ARGUMENTUM

Adolescens ingenuus literarum pertaesus acrem militiam parat, libros loricis, galeis, ensibus mutare cogitat: eum Doctor nullis argumentis dimovere ab instituta ratione potest. Secum ducit alium adolescentem, cui odium literarum persuaserat. Militarem in modum ornati dum viam ineunt, obvios habent duos milites fugitivos, sibi olim non ignotos, vestitu laceros, esuritione confectos, et illuvie immundos. Horum oratione vitam castrensem insectantium, ac deplorantium, ut qui in re praesenti fuerint, adolescentes ambo sic permoventur, ut vestigia relegant, et ad studia contempta, ac deserta revertantur.

ARGUMENTUM (II, ex appendice)

Adolescens pertaesus literarum cogitat militiam. Eum Magister nullis rationibus a suspecto consilio revocare potest. Adiungit ille sibi alium adolescentem: qui cum ornatu militari in viam se dat. Incidit in fugitivos milites duos habitu et squalore deformes ac laceros, quorum oratione statum illum vitae deplorantium ac detestantium commoventur ambo, ut ad studia sese recipiant. Sed illorum fugitivorum alter sperans coniugi se optatum esse reversurum, quam cum parvis liberis ab amicis de re familiari

PLOT SUMMARY

An aristocratic young man, fed up with his studies, gets ready for harsh military service, and contemplates exchanging his books for breastplates, helmets and swords. His teacher is unable to dissuade him from his resolution with any arguments whatsoever. The young noble takes along with him another young man who has also been convinced to hate his studies. Decked out in military style they begin their journey, and then meet two deserting soldiers, who were once their acquaintances, with tattered clothing, bodies used up by hunger, and filthy with grime. When these two inveigh against camp life and deplore it, since they have just been in it themselves, the two young men are so moved that they retrace their steps and go back to the studies they had spurned and deserted.

PLOT SUMMARY (II, from appendix)

An aristocratic young man, fed up with his studies, contemplates military service. His teacher is unable by any reasoning to call him back him from the path he has embarked upon. The young man enlists another youth who commits himself to the journey, dressed in military garb, and he happens upon two deserting soldiers, unsightly and ill-used both in their dress and in their hygiene. Both young men are so moved by the deserters' remarks deploring and reviling their lot in life inopem deseruerat, verbis et verberibus male accipitur, vixque impetrare potest, ut sibi peccatum condonetur secumque in gratiam redeat.

PERSONAE

STRATOCLES ex studioso miles.
EUBULUS Magister.
POLEMIUS alter studiosus, miles.
TREMONIUS
MISOMACHUS fugitivi milites.
FAUSTINA uxor Misomachi

that they return to their studies. One of the deserters, however, hopes to be welcomed back by the wife and small children he had deserted and left penniless and bereft of friends. She gives him a nasty reception, with verbal and corporal abuse, and he barely manages to have his sin forgiven and to return to her good graces.

CHARACTERS

Stratocles, once a student, now a soldier
Eubulus, a teacher
Polemius, another former student and now soldier
Tremonius, a soldier AWOL (a deserter)
Misomachus, a soldier AWOL (a deserter)
Faustina, Misomachus' wife

STRATOCLES sive BELLUM

I.

Stratocles discipulus, Eubulus praeceptor.

Stratocles

Vidi ego, et audivi, et lectitavi saepius
Varia cruciamenta, doloresque maxumos,
Quos in maleficos solet expendere carnifex.
Verum hercle verum, haud est talis molestia,
Nullus eculeus, catasta nulla, nulla crux,   5
Nullum tormentum Phalaridis, aut Mezentii
Cum studiosorum poenis conferri potest.
Illi demum mortales sunt miserrimi,
Illi omnium miserorum sunt miserrimi,
Nec ulla est gens in toto orbe aerumnosior.   10
Paucis annis fit sutor, sartor optimus,
Lanius, pistor, pastor, fictor, lictor, cocus,
Figulus, faber, piscator, carbonarius,
Usurarius, olearius, vitriarius,
Fullo, canicida, interpollator, pellio: 15
Isti, inquam, clari artifices evadunt brevi:
Nobis ante obitum doctis fieri non licet.
Mors quando adveniens sera pulsat ostium,
Tunc primum aspicimus, sed procul, sapientiam.
Natura nobis tunc noverca dicitur.   20
Sexcentos, credo, annos largiri debuit,

STRATOCLES or WAR

Act I

[Stratocles, student, and Eubulus, teacher, before the school]

Stratocles[1]

Many times have I seen, and heard, and read about the different
tortures and the greatest pains that an executioner is accustomed
to pay out to criminals.[2] By Hercules! There is no way any evil
like this can be compared to the punishments of students – no 5
wooden rack, no gallows, no cross, no torture of Phalaris or of
Mezentius.[3] Students especially are the most miserable people.
They are the most miserable of all miserable people. There are
no people in the whole world more miserable.   10

Within a few years you can become a superior cobbler, tailor,
butcher, baker, shepherd, sculptor, bodyguard, cook, potter,
carpenter, fisherman, coal miner, banker, oil-seller, glass-worker,
fuller,[4] animal handler, polisher, fur dealer: those very people, 15
I say, turn out as reputable craftsmen in only a short time.
But we students aren't even allowed to become wise before
death.[5] When late-arriving death knocks on the door, then we
behold wisdom for the first time, but from a distance, and the 20
one we used to call gentle Mother Nature we then call an evil
stepmother.[6] She should have bestowed upon us six-hundred

Quibus literati bonas horas male perderent.
Fluxerunt anni plus, opinor, quindecim,
Cum me pater applicavit ad istas literas,
Ex illo discendo minus quam nihil scio.   25
O rem iocosam, et ridiculariam affatim.
Quadam in schola sedisse quendam praedicant
Lapideum auditorem toto septennio.
Ego sum οὗτος ἐκεῖνος. Ut valide trivi asserem!
Orbilius noster valde plagosus homo erat,   30
Meum saepe in ruborem mihi corium dedit,
Saepe haud sedere quivi prae vibicibus.
Ita puerile scinditur corpusculum.
Omnes parietes fletu et flagris personant.
Ecce studiorum bellissima primordia.   35
Grammaticam quid deinde sequitur? Poetica.
Ista Poetica nihil est sacratius.
Montes et fontes, Musas, et Apollinem
Colunt poetae: hinc versus tam dulces fluunt.
Quingenta carminum illis genera, Dii boni.   40
Mendaciorum quas appellant fabulas,
Trecenta plaustra. Troporum dena millia.
Ineptiarum numerus infinitus est.
Hic etiam fuit haerendum multo tempore,
In Herculeis laboribus, et Atlanticis.   45
Domina Calliope, quam esse narrant virginem
(Si virgo est, quae Linumque, Rhesumque peperit)
Quamvis rogata, si memini, plus millies,
Favere non vult. Nec favebo illi amplius:
Immo medium digitum mulieri porrigam.   50
Rhetor etiam fui totum quadriennium.
Quod didici? accipite uno verbo: nihil, nihil!
Exordiorum ibi aspexi ingentem struem,
Epilogorum longissimas ibi series.
Brevi complectar caetera. Et Logicus fui,   55
Soloecismos pro syllogismis condidi.
Quid tum? quasi hunc morem primus introduxerim.
Nunc sum philosophus amplius sexennium.
(Vos supputate, si annos retuli quindecim)
Hoc me studium quam miseris vexavit modis!   60

years,[7] I believe, in which the "learned" could squander their good time.

More than fifteen years have passed, I reckon, since my father steered me to those books, and from that education I know 25 less than nothing. What a humorous and absolutely hilarious situation! They say that in a certain school a certain student sat petrified for a whole seven years.[8] That student — *c'est moi!*[9] I wore the varnish right off the bench![10]

Our grammar teacher Orbilius was a man passionately 30 fond of flogging.[11] He often beat my hide red; often I could hardly sit because of the welts. That's how boys' poor bodies are beaten.[12] All the walls resound with cries and cracks. What a 35 lovely commencement to our studies.

What then follows grammar?[13] Poetry. Nothing is more sacred than that very poetry. The poets worship mountains and fountains, and the Muses and Apollo:[14] thence flow verses so sweet. They have five hundred kinds of poems, for goodness' 40 sake; three hundred wagon-loads of lies which they call stories; ten thousand figures of speech; an infinite number of absurdities. Here, too, we were stuck for a long time on the 45 labors of Hercules and Atlas. Lady Calliope,[15] allegedly a virgin (a "virgin" who gave birth to both Linus and Rhesus),[16] although I have asked her over a thousand times, if I remember correctly, chooses not to smile upon me. So I won't smile at her any more: 50 on the contrary, I will extend my middle finger to the broad.[17]

I was also an orator for four whole years.[18] What did I learn? Understand it in a single word: nada, nothing! I looked here at an enormous pile of introductions, and there at an endless series of conclusions. I will briefly sum up the rest. I was also a student 55 of logic, but I composed solecisms instead of syllogisms.[19] What next? As if I have to tell you this is how we do things![20] And I've been a philosopher for more than six years now. (All of you, do the math, whether I went back fifteen years).[21] In what 60 wretched ways this studying has vexed me! What sobs it has

Quos peperit singultus, et quot suspiria!
Ut crebras misero saepe excivit lacrymas!
Produxi ad multam noctem saepe vigilias,
Et incaenatus discessi saepe cubitum.
Legi, relegi paginam unam centies,   65
Non rem magis exsculpsi, quam ex pumicibus aquam.
Ut Aristoteli isti mala cadant quam plurima,
Qui noluit a nobis sua scripta intellegi.
Ne vivam, si homini illi non effoderem oculos,
Siquidem ipse mihi effodit prope cerebrum.   70
Nihil est sapientibus istis insipientius,
Qui cum ventosi nosse iactent omnia,
Divina, humana, supera, media et infima,
Quis extiterit stultorum primus nesciunt.
Haec et alia mecum plura cum considero,   75
Literarum studiis nil videtur vanius,
Morosius, crudelius, inhumanius.
Vires debilitant, succum membris detrahunt,
Pallorem inducunt vultibus, ut cadaverum,
Capitis dolorem, tussim, maciem, atque scabiem,   80
Morbos perennes, extremam ignorantiam.
Deinde parentes ad paupertatem protrahunt,
Quia sustentantur intolerandis sumptibus,
At publicae rei nec hilum commodant,
Quae non libris, potius armis defenditur.   85
Nunc ergo hoc mihi visum est factu longe optimum,
Studiis istis ut ergo remittam nuntium,
Ac recta militatum proficiscar aliquo:
Nam hic vitam perdo, gloriam, et pecuniam.
Hoc facere certum est, ita me amabunt caelites.   90
Vade liber pessime, alium tibi quaere dominum:
Si rebitas ad me, in latrinis faxo iaceas.
Atat, quaenam haec barba est, quae istinc prodit foras?
Praeceptor est. Scio probe, quid sibi velit:
Etsi quid ipse acturus sit, nec dum sciat.   95
Frequenter abesse a ludo sollenne est meum,
Atque in caupona perpotare ad vesperam,
Ut hodie diligentes discipuli solent.
Ea caussa me quaesitum processit domo.

produced, and how many sighs! How constant were the tears it often roused in me, wretch that I am![22] And frequently I held long vigils late into the night. I often went off to bed without supper. I read and reread a single page a hundred times, but 65 I wrung out nothing more from it than water from a stone.[23] Would that as many evils as possible befall that Aristotle, who didn't wish us to understand his writings. Let me die, if I can't gouge out that man's eyes, since in fact he himself nearly gouged 70 out my brain. Nothing is less intelligent than those intellectuals, those blowhards who, although they boast that they know all things divine, human, lofty, middling and lowly, don't know who the inventor of idiocy was.[24]

When I myself think about this and many other things, 75 it seems that nothing is more futile, more painstaking, more unforgiving, more inhuman than the humanities.[25] These studies sap students of their strength, suck the life from their limbs, and drain the color from their faces, just like a corpse. They bring on headaches, coughs, emaciation and eczema, endless illness, and 80 extreme ignorance.

On top of that, they reduce parents to poverty, since they consume outrageous sums, while not returning a single thing to the commonwealth, which is protected not by books, but rather 85 by arms. So now this seems to me by far the best thing to do: to renounce those studies and to depart straightaway for military service anywhere else. For here I am ruining my life, destroying my glory, and wasting my money.[26] I am determined to do 90 this, heaven preserve me. Get lost, foulest book, find yourself another owner: if you return to me, I'll make sure you lie in the latrine.[27]

[*Enter Eubulus*]

Well, well, who's this bearded fellow coming out from there? If it isn't our teacher. I know exactly what he wants, even if he 95 himself doesn't know yet what he'll do. I religiously skip school and attend the tavern to drink into the evening,[28] as today's diligent students regularly do. That's the reason he's left home to search for me.

Mirabitur, de bello quando audiverit. 100

EUBULUS
Salvus sis, Stratocle!

STRATOCLES
                    Et tu per me salvus sies.

EUBULUS
Quid solus hic tecum es locutus tamdiu?
Ubinam vagatus continuos dies novem?
Quid molitus? Cur non dedisti mihi operam?
Responde, quid taces? 105

STRATOCLES
                    Edictabo tibi
Quod res est, ut sciens sis quam planissime:
Non iam discere lubet, bellare lubet magis,
Rotare enses, telis, et ferro ludere.
Satisne aperte dictum? ecquid me intelligis?

EUBULUS
Propemodum, Stratocle. Pro deum atque hominum fidem, 110
Quid audio?

STRATOCLES
          Quod verum est.

EUBULUS
                    Verum?

STRATOCLES
                         Verissimum.

EUBULUS
Dormitas adolescens, loqueris per somnium.

He'll be stunned when he hears about the war.   100

EUBULUS

    I trust you are well, Stratocles!

STRATOCLES

    I trust you are, as well.

EUBULUS

    Why have you been talking to yourself alone here for such a
long time? Where in the world have you been wandering for
nine whole days? What have you been doing? Why haven't you
paid attention to me? Answer, why are you so silent?   105

STRATOCLES

    I'll lecture[29] you on the subject, so that you know it as plainly
as possible. I no longer feel like learning. I much prefer to fight,
to brandish the double-edged sword, to play with the javelin
and the dagger. Have I made myself clear enough? Do you
understand me at all?

EUBULUS

    Just about, Stratocles. For the love of gods and men, what 110
am I hearing?

STRATOCLES

    The truth.

EUBULUS

    The truth?

STRATOCLES

    The absolute truth!

EUBULUS

    You are dreaming, young man: you are talking in your sleep.

STRATOCLES
Non sum in schola: vigilo, et vigilans fabulor.

EUBULUS
Id est quod puto: te mihi narrare fabulam.

STRATOCLES
Quod ipsus facit, omnes facere hoc existimat: 115
Dies et annos fabulatur fabulas.
Rem dixi, Eubule, si credis, credas licet.
Si non credideris, ego credam, nil te moror.

EUBULUS
Ergone tu in bellum?

STRATOCLES
                    Certe.

EUBULUS
                              Quid monstri tu alis?
Quasi hic ad te tumulandum humus non suppetat.   120
Canibus et volucribus vis dare convivium?
Refer sine fuco, mi Stratocle, quid cogites.
Pugnamne?

STRATOCLES
            Pugnam.

EUBULUS
                        Caedes?

STRATOCLES
                                Caedes.

STRATOCLES

I'm not in class: I'm wide awake, and I'm telling you this with my eyes wide open.

EUBULUS

This is what I think: you are telling me tall tales.[30]

STRATOCLES

[*Aside*] Whatever he does, he thinks everyone does the same. 115
He's been telling tall tales every day for years.

[*Addresses Eubulus*] I've told you how it stands, Eubulus, believe it if you want. Even if you won't, I will, and I'm not stopping you.

EUBULUS

And so you're off to war?

STRATOCLES

Certainly.

EUBULUS

What sort of nightmare are you nurturing? As if there is not 120
enough earth here for burying you! Do you wish to provide a feast for dogs and vultures as well?[31] Tell me without deceit[32] what you are thinking, my Stratocles. Battle?

STRATOCLES

Battle.

EUBULUS

Slaughter?

STRATOCLES

Slaughter.

EUBULUS

Vulnera?

STRATOCLES
Vulnera.

EUBULUS

Iamne igitur penitus statuisti mori?

STRATOCLES
Videte, ut mortem pertimescant philosophi.   125
Mori non equidem statui, sed viriliter
Stare in acie, ac hostilem elicere sanguinem,
Et hac multos dextra sub Orcum mittere.

EUBULUS
Quam inviti credimus, quod factum nolumus.
Dic age. Tu literas deserere fixum habes?   130

STRATOCLES
Habeo.

EUBULUS

Tu castra tendis, et Martem sequi?

STRATOCLES
Ita, ita, ita: hem quoties iam sum confessus tibi?

EUBULUS
Sanusne es?

STRATOCLES

Sanissimus. An ad bella veniunt
Etiam aegroti?

EUBULUS
Wounds?

STRATOCLES
Wounds.

EUBULUS
So, have you now deep down decided on death?

STRATOCLES
[*Aside*] Look at how the philosophers are all terrified of 125
death.
[*Addresses Eubulus*] I have certainly not decided to die, but to
stand like a man in the ranks and spill enemy blood and send
many of them down to Hades with this right hand.[33]

EUBULUS
How unwilling we are to believe anything that we don't want
to see happen.[34] Well then, tell me your plan. Have you resolved 130
to desert your studies?

STRATOCLES
I have.

EUBULUS
Are you setting a course for the barracks, and following Mars?

STRATOCLES
Yes, yes, yes: look, how many times have I told you this
already?

EUBULUS
Are you feeling well?

STRATOCLES
Perfectly well. Or do sick people go to battle too?

EUBULUS

        Haud istuc rogo.

STRATOCLES

                  Dic quid roges.

EUBULUS

Sanusne mentis es?   135

STRATOCLES

            Apage sis, qui me tuis
Insanum verbis concinnare postulas.
Fui insanus, qui aetatem egi in literis.
Quod stulte feci, nunc sapienter corrigo.
Sapio, quanquam sero, et reduco calculum.

EUBULUS

O Stratocle, o Stratocle, ausculta paulisper tuum   140
Praeceptorem, qui fidus tibi semper fuit,
Qui te dilexit ceu germanum filium.

STRATOCLES

Quaecunque animus fert, loquere, promptus audiam.

EUBULUS

Primum omnium labores cur perdas tuos
Tot annis positos in praeclaris artibus?   145
Praesertim cum non mediocres effeceris
Progressus, idque nostro testimonio,
Quibus per philosophiam nec mentiri integrum est,
Nec palpari aliquem, ut est moris adulantium.
Subita consilia raro sunt faelicia.   150
Cur istuc aures est praetervectum tuas,
Quod vulgus iactare solet in proverbio?
Tria esse, quae deliberanda sint diu:
Profiteri monachum, ducere uxorem domum,
Et, quod praecipuum, militiae nomen dare.   155

EUBULUS

That is not what I mean.

STRATOCLES

Then tell me what you do mean.

EUBULUS

Are you well in the head?   135

STRATOCLES

Get away from here, please, since you're trying to make me
insane with your words.[35] I *was* insane to spend my youth
studying. What I did foolishly, now I correct wisely.[36] I have
become wise, though late, so now I correct my error.[37]

[handwritten: would a wise person really say that?]

EUBULUS

O Stratocles, Stratocles, pay attention for a little while to 140
your teacher, for I have always been true to you and loved you
like my very own son.

STRATOCLES

Wherever the spirit leads you, speak, and I'll listen willingly.

EUBULUS

First of all, why are you wasting the effort that you've put for
so many years into the noble arts? Especially since you have 145
made no middling progress (and that is my personal judgment),
and it is necessary for philosophers such as myself neither to lie
nor to flatter, as is the habit of sycophants. Rash decisions are 150
rarely successful. Why has the proverb, which the masses are
wont to toss about, gone in one ear and out the other? There are
three things which ought to be considered at length: to enter a
monastery, to take a wife, and, chief among them, to enlist in 155
the military.[38]

[handwritten: — someone who feigns obedience to gain advantage]

Nunc te, mi Stratocle, per tuum genium obsecro,
Ut de re tam ardua amplius deliberes.
Noli exspectare, dum te eventus monuerit.
Eventus namque stultorum magister est.
Dispice paulum, quot incommoda Mars afferat.   160
Principio, quod erat libertatis proprium,
Id funditus sublatum est: vivere ut velis.
Ducum imperia pro lege habenda sunt tibi.
Pugnare vis, manere te in castris iubent.
Excedere praelio cupis, pergere iubent.   165
Exuvias, et spolia vis legere, illi vetant.
Nisi obedias, repente suffigunt cruci.
Vitam hominis atque belluae iuxta aestimant.
Excubiae sunt agendae in noctes singulas,
Vivendum ex rapto, esuries patienda, et sitis,   170
Bibendum flumen turbidum, et panis niger
Vorandus, ipso ferro et chalybe durior,
Longissima pedibus conficienda intinera.
Menses in multos non dabitur stipendium:
Nec minus eo laboris imperabitur.   175
In tergo etiam numismata cudentur tuo.
Ecquid probatam ducis hanc pecuniam?

STRATOCLES
Verbera gratis ego inveniam quam facillime.

EUBULUS
Quid de squalore dicam, quid de sordibus?
Quid de vermiculis, immo de pediculis?   180
Quorum catervas densas milites alunt.
Tonsoribus haud utuntur, tondent mutuum
Pulcherrime: namque enses sunt novaculae.
Quibus abradunt cum crinibus totum caput.
Crebro item e venis mittunt putrem sanguinem.   185
Sed (quod parum salutiferum medici canunt)
Venas recludunt, et resecant multas simul.
STRATOCLES
Tales chirurgos nunquam ego mihi optaverim.

Now I beseech you, my Stratocles, in the name of your soul, to think more fully about such a serious matter. Do not wait for that experience to instruct you, for experience is the teacher of fools.[39]

Ponder for a moment how many troubles Mars brings. To 160 begin with, what was characteristic of freedom has been uprooted from its foundation: to live as you might wish. You must consider the generals' orders to be law. You wish to fight, they order you to remain in camp. You desire to retreat from 165 battle, they order you to charge. You wish to gather plunder and spoils, they forbid it. Should you disobey, straightaway they fasten you to a cross.[40] They value the life of man and beast equally. Standing sentry duty every single night; living 170 off plunder; suffering hunger and thirst; drinking muddy river water; bolting down black bread, harder than iron itself and steel; completing the longest marches on foot. For months on end there will be no salary paid, nor will any less work be 175 assigned. Coins will even be struck on your back. Is this what you call legitimate coinage?[41]

STRATOCLES

I can already get beatings quite easily for free.

EUBULUS

What should I say about squalor and about filth? What about maggots, and moreover what about lice? Soldiers nourish full 180 squadrons of them. They do not use barbers: they barber one another most handsomely, for their swords are their razors. They use these to scrape off the whole scalp along with the hair. They frequently let putrid blood from their veins as well. But as they open the veins, they cut through many others at the same 185 time (which the doctors declare is not very healthy).

STRATOCLES

I for one would never pick surgeons[42] like that.

EUBULUS
Heu quantos aestus, quam atrox frigus sustinent!
Pro delicatis pellibus arma horrida gerunt.   190
Arma aenea, et ipso pondere quam gravissima.
Sub aetheris axe nudo quid non perferunt!
Omnes molestias, omnes iniurias,
Pluvias, nives, tonitrua, nimbos, grandines,
Fulgura, fulmina, ventos, procellas, turbines.   195
Iam quoties morbi grassantur in exercitum?
Quam saepe castra invadit pestilentia!
Adhaec in bello pro quantum casus valet!
Communis Mars, bellorum incertus exitus.
Cadunt magnanimi, timidi sunt superstites.   200
Victorem quoties vis fortunae perculit,
Tergumque victis dare coegit improba!
Age vero, interfectis quisnam funus facit?
Ubinam amicorum moesta comploratio?
(Hoc siquidem non negligendum duxit Solon,   205
Vacare fletu qui non vult mortem suam.)
Esto autem quis fiat redux in patriam,
Deum immortalem, quam deformatus redit!
Cicatricibus insignis horrendum in modum,
Plenus dorsus, pleni pedes, plenum caput,   210
Mutilata facies amputatis auribus,
Praetruncatus nasus inhonesto vulnere.
Interea coniux alteri nupsit viro,
Aut quaestum fecit prostituto corpore:
Nati vivunt aliena misericordia.   215
Si forte redeat illaesus membra omnia,
Contemnit populus omnis, et pro ignavo habet.
O quam exploratum succinit paroemia:
Bellum dulce est inexpertis. Dicas mihi,
Tune igitur nullum vis unquam bellum geri?   220
Vis nos inermes hostibus dare iugulum?
Minime volo: est quando bellum geri expedit,
Et vero debet: sed te, similes ac tui
Adolescentes, praestanti mactos indole,
Columina familiae, egregium decus urbium,   225
Hos, inquam, a castris abstinendos autumo.

EUBULUS

Alas, how much heat and what fierce cold they endure![43]
Instead of soft furs they wear bristling arms — arms of unyielding 190
bronze, and also in their weight very hard to bear.[44] What do
they not suffer under the axis of heaven! All the troubles, all
the injuries, rain, snow, thunder, clouds, hail-storms, lightning,
thunder-bolts, winds, gales, and tornadoes. And now how often 195
does disease plague the army? How often pestilence invades
the camp!

In addition to these things, how strong chance is in war!
Mars is impartial, and the end of wars uncertain.[45] Brave men 200
fall, while the timid survive. How often the power of fortune
strikes down the victor, and shamelessly forces him to flee from
those he has conquered. Moreover, who in the world performs
the burials for those slain abroad? Where in the world is the
mournful lamentation of friends? Even Solon, who restricted 205
lavish funeral expenses, thought that this should not be neglected,
since he did not want his own death to be without tears.[46]

Should, however, someone happen to return to the fatherland,[47]
Immortal God, how disfigured he returns! How "distinguished"
he is by scars to a horrible degree, his back full of them, his 210
feet full of them, his head full of them, and his face mutilated,
his ears amputated, his nose hacked off: shameful wounds.[48]
Meanwhile, his wife has married another man, or earned money
by prostituting her body, and his children live off a stranger's 215
pity.[49] Should he by chance return uninjured with everything
intact, the whole community scorns him, and considers him a
coward. O how true the proverb rings: *Bellum dulce est inexpertis*
— War is sweet to the inexperienced.[50]

Would you say to me, "Do you therefore wish that war never 220
be waged? Do you wish that we bare our throats defenselessly
to the enemy?" I want nothing of the sort. There is a time when
waging war is useful, and indeed necessary:[51] but you, and young
men like you, blessed with outstanding innate excellence,[52] are
the pillars of your families, the supreme glory of your cities. 225
These young men, I say, must be kept from the barracks. For

Quapropter, Stratocle, si quis est precibus locus,
Muta consilium in melius, et hanc mentem exue.
Quod tibi suadeo, meo suaderem filio.
Fallit te sententia, non rectam instas viam.   230

STRATOCLES
Tua dicta, Eubule, nec tantillum me movent;
Ventis trado. Coeptis nequeo desistere.
Sive mihi mens iniecta est haec divinitus:
Sive potius mea mihi cupido fit Deus –
Clare sonantem exaudio taratantaram,   235
Micantes cerno clypeos, et gladios truces.
Nobile facinus, certando vitam amittere:
Effaeminatum, in pluma, et in rosa emori.
Carebo sepulchro? nullo virtus indiget.
Et quisquis urnam non habet, hunc caelum tegit.   240
Tu cupiebas magnum me fieri philosophum,
Factus sum, vitam et mortem contemno pariter,
Opes irrideo, dura possum perpeti.
Amo patriam, cui consecro meum sanguinem.
Haec quicunque didicit, eruditus est satis,   245
Atque haud inutilis patriae civis alitur.
Quis autem est hominum, qui vivat sine legibus?
Qui plane nullius imperio sit subditus?
Malo imperare mihi fortissimum ducem
In castris, quam turpem domi socordiam.   250
Porro animosum nunquam oderit dux militem:
Ignavum, ut tu discipulum, non potest pati.
Sitis, fames, paupertas, aestus, frigora,
Omnia virtutis isthaec instrumenta sunt.
Maior apud vos pediculorum messis est.   255
Etiam in mediis morbi vagantur urbibus,
Saevaque pestilitas civitates opprimit.
Nec vos ab omnibus exempti estis casibus.
Iam quod cicatricum bene completa facies
Deformis apparet tibi, quam ridiculus es!   260
Turpia dices monumenta fortitudinis?
Et te tantopere pulcher aspectus capit?
Mihi quidem ob vulnera crebra consutum caput

this reason, Stratocles, if there is any place for prayer, change
your plan for the better and cast off this resolution. This I urge
you, as I would urge my own son. Your plan deceives you; you
pursue the wrong path.   230

STRATOCLES

Your words, Eubulus, do not move me the least bit; I cast
them to the winds. I cannot stop what I've started.[53] Either my
intention has been divinely inspired, or rather my own desire is
becoming God for me.[54]

I hear the unmistakable blare of the trumpet.[55] I see the 235
shining of shields, and savage swords. 'Tis a noble deed,[56] to
forfeit thy life in the fray: womanish, to die on pillows and rose
petals.[57] Will I be without a tomb? Bravery needs none. And
whoever has no coffin, the heavens cover him. You wanted 240
me to become a great philosopher, and I have become one.
I scorn life and death equally; I scoff at riches; I am able to
bear the full measure of hardships.[58] I love my fatherland, to
which I dedicate my blood. Whoever has learned these things 245
is educated enough, and the fatherland has raised a citizen by
no means useless.

But is there any man who can live without laws? Who
is subject to absolutely no one's authority? I would rather a
man of decisive action[59] command me in the barracks, than 250
disgraceful sloth at home. Furthermore, a leader never hates a
brave and dutiful soldier; but a sluggish one, just like you with
your students, he cannot tolerate. Thirst, hunger, poverty, heat,
cold, all these are the makings of manliness.[60]

As for lice, the harvest is more abundant among all of you. 255
And diseases spread unchecked even in the middle of cities,[61]
and a savage plague overwhelms whole countries.[62] None of
you here is exempt from every accident.[63]

And how absurd you are, that a face all covered with scars 260
appears deformed to you. Will you call these marks of valor
disgraceful? Does a handsome appearance captivate you that
much? A head stitched up because of numerous wounds,

Consutae malae, frons, et nares denique
Gratissimam videntur praeferre faciem.   265
Uxorem non duxi, non genui liberos,
Nihil timendum interea, quid fiat domi.
Bellum est in votis, in bello mihi omnia.
Ad bellum currere mei gestiunt pedes.

EUBULUS
Et ad haec dicturus quid tandem est senex pater?   270
Quid pia mater, cui tu unico es magis unicus?
Parentes ante obitum cur sic orbos facis?
Cur illis de te tam ingentes luctus cies?
Non me, putas, iratus obiurget pater?
Non a me repetat filium cum iurgio?   275
Non clamet: "Redde natum, redde liberos,
Quos fidei iam pridem commiseram tuae"?
Quid contra fabor, mi Stratocle? "Arrogans fuit,
Superbus, confidens, protervus, contumax,
Meos explosit monitus pertinaciter.   280
Amanter hominem collocutus, omnia
Tentavi, me miserum habuit ludibrio:
Non potuimus mentem expugnare ferream"?

STRATOCLES
Facessant oro lamenta, et querimoniae:
Quamvis caelum ruat, non aliud statuero.   285
Ac iam iam, si parumper hic me manseris,
Reversus apparebo ornatu militis.

EUBULUS
Nihil ago, exspectabo tamen, actutum redi.
Hodie experior, si quidquam expertus sum prius,
Ad veritatis ut bene collimet scopum,   290
Rebus qui scripsit geminis averti a bono
Iuventutum: imprudentia atque viribus.
Istis nam elati, audent bellum capessere:

stitched-up cheeks, forehead, and even a stitched-up nose seem,
to me at least, to present a most pleasing face. I have not taken 265
a wife, nor have I sired sons, so I have nothing to fear at home.
War is in my prayers, war is my everything. My feet are eager
to run to war.

EUBULUS

And to all this, what then will your aged father say? What 270
about your devoted mother, for whom you are the one and only?
Why are you making your parents childless like this before they
die? Why are you provoking them to such enormous grief over
you? Do you think your father will not abuse me in his anger?
That he will not demand his son back from me with abusive 275
language? That he will not shout, "Return my son,[64] return my
children, since I had entrusted them to your faithful care a long
time ago now?" What shall I say in reply, my Stratocles? This?
"He was presumptuous, arrogant, hubristic, reckless, defiant,
and he obstinately rejected my warnings. Although I spoke 280
affectionately to the man and tried everything, he considered
me a laughingstock, even though I was miserable. I was not
able to conquer his unyielding will."

STRATOCLES

I beg you, let the laments and complaints stop. Although
the sky may fall, I will not decide any differently. And right 285
now, if you wait for me here just a moment, I will reappear fully
outfitted as a soldier.

EUBULUS

I am having no effect, nevertheless I will await you: come
right back. [*Exit Stratocles*]
Today I am putting it to the test, if I have ever put
anything to the test before, how well the writer hit the target 290
of truth,[65] who wrote that the young are led astray from the
good by twin things: imprudence and their own strength.[66]
Carried away by the latter, they dare to head off to war;

Illa impediti, quod frugiferum est, non vident.
Nec admiratione est quidquam dignius   295
Adolescente in quo eluceat prudentia:
Facilius est corvum reperire candidum.
Qui stultos dixerit omnes, errabit parum.
Inde est quod sapiens sapienter sanxit Solon,
Ut ne iuvenes aliquem magistratum gerant,   300
Neu consiliis unquam adhibeantur publicis.
Aetas iuvenilis est inconstantis animi,
Levi momento huc illuc mox impellitur:
Et cum quovis flectatur non aegerrime,
In vitium, ut cera, flectitur facillime.   305
Innumeras volvit secum semper ineptias,
Noctu diuque continenter somniat.
De consequentibus malis, de funere,
Deque senectute nequit audire verbulum.
Omnes delicias, et voluptates amat.   310
Canibus, et equis alendis gaudet maxime.
Festivis interest avide spectaculis.
Potat libenter, et bene ludit aleam.
Spernit Iunonem, spernit ipsam Palladem:
Ac Venerem multo pulchriorem iudicat.   315
Non etenim diligit valde sapientiam.
Nil est sollicita ut magnas sibi congerat opes.
Molles risus, et molles sermonum iocos,
Et strepitum citharae amplectitur supra modum.
Monitores aspernatur, et prorsus fugit.   320
Minatur damna, et exilium censoribus.
Iras et animum in fronte et ore gestitat.
Loquacula est, et tantum praebet, quantum habet.
Maioris non sunt uspiam spes et fides.
Credit iuventus multum, sperat omnia.   325
Suis amica nimium est laudatoribus.
Quicunque vero illius studia non colunt,
Cum huiusmodi nullam societatem coit.
Iniurias placato animo haud sciunt pati,
Eas quam possunt vindicant acerrime.   330
Inducere illos ad fraudem nullus labor:
In hora circumscribuntur vel centies.

hindered by the former, they do not see what is profitable.

Nor is there anything more worthy of admiration than a 295
young man in whom wisdom shines forth: it is easier to find
a white raven.[67] He who says they are all fools will be only
a little off the mark.[68] That is the origin of what sage Solon
sagaciously sanctioned, specifically that young men never hold 300
public office, and that they never be consulted about any public
issues. A young man's years are marked by a capricious mind,
which is driven here and there by the slightest influence. Since
it bends without resistance (like wax) however you wish, it is
bent very easily toward vice.[69] He constantly turns innumerable 305
absurdities over in his mind, and day and night he dreams
continuously.[70] About evil consequences, about burial, and
about old age, he is unable to hear a single word. He loves 310
every indulgence and pleasure. His greatest joy is raising dogs
and horses.[71] He greedily takes part in holiday spectacles. He
drinks liberally, and plays dice well. He scorns Juno, and he
even scorns Athena, and he judges Venus far more attractive.[72] 315
And the fact is he does not love wisdom greatly. He is not
anxious to accumulate great riches for himself. Gentle laughter,
and flirtatious[73] jokes in conversation, and the murmur of a lute:
he embraces all of these far too much.

He despises teachers and puts them to flight. He threatens 320
those who censor him with injuries and exile. He wears his
anger and feelings on his forehead and face. He is loquacious
and unrestrained.[74] At no other time are his hopes or his faith in
others higher.[75] A young man is overly[76] trusting and hopes for 325
everything. He is too fond of those who praise him. Whoever
does not share his interests is not admitted into his company.
They scarcely know how to tolerate insults with equanimity,
and avenge them as bitterly as they can. It is no great task to 330
introduce them to deceit:[77] you can fool[78] them 100 times in an
hour.

Haec aetas denique incerta, et multum est vaga,
Mutationibus subiecta plurimis,
Iamque huc propendet, iam illuc, iam alio respicit,   335
Nec quis adolescentis futurus exitus,
Quis terminus, bonus an malus, dici potest.

Explodit bombardulam egrediens Stratocles.

STRATOCLES
Magister, syllogismus hic dexter fuit,
In posterum tales facturum spondeo.
Educit pugionem.

Haec maior propositio: isthaec erit minor: 340

Educit gladium.

Haec conclusio, quae rem consummatam dabit.
Dic mihi, Eubule, placetne hic tibi ornatus novus?
Meo iudicio non fui venustior.

EUBULUS
Meo iudicio non fuisti turpior.
Caligae sunt dissectae, dissectus calceus,   345
Dissectus thorax. Scin' quid haec praesagiant?

STRATOCLES
Quidnam?

EUBULUS
          Tuum corpus ita dissecabitur.

STRATOCLES
Non hercle, quin multos prius dissecuerim,
Et gladium hunc tepidis condiderim in pulmonibus.

In short, this age is uncertain, and is considerably unsettled, subject to multitudinous changes. First he is inclined here, now 335 there, now he looks elsewhere. Whatever the outcome of a young man, whatever his end, good or bad, no one can say.[79]

[*Stratocles enters dressed as a soldier and fires a large weapon*][80]

STRATOCLES
Teacher, this was the right syllogism.
In the future, I vow to use ones like this.
[*Draws a dagger*]
This is the major proposition; [*Slashes air with dagger*]   340
over there will be the minor.
[*Draws a sword; slashes air a second time*].

This is the conclusion, which will solve everything.[81] Tell me, Eubulus, do you like my new gear? In my judgment, I've never been more charming.

EUBULUS
In *my* judgment, you have never been more repulsive. Your boots are tattered, your shoes torn to pieces, and your breastplate 345 skewered.[82] Do you not know what these portend?

STRATOCLES
What?

EUBULUS
Thus will your own body be tattered, torn, and skewered.

STRATOCLES
No, by Hercules, not before I have skewered many first and sheathed this sword in their warm lungs.

EUBULUS
Formido, ne Mars iam nunc in lingua siet: 350
Postquam instabit conflictus, recidat in pedes,
Ac tu fugitor magnus fias pro milite.

STRATOCLES
Dii meliora. Eubule, istuc noli edicere,
Quinimmo victorem multarum gentium,
Opimis indutum spoliis, si dii adiuvant,   355
Visurus es aliquando Stratoclem.

EUBULUS
                              Scilicet
Multis onustum vulneribus, et sceleribus
Ego videbo. Sed te per caput oro tuum,
Et quidquid in hac vita tibi est charissimum,
Te circumspice, saltemque ad punctum temporis   360
Prudentem cogitationem suspice,
Mi Stratocle: ne tantum dolorem inusseris
Parentibus, quorum perit solatium
Te amisso. Per Divos omnes quaeso, rogo,
Per caelum, et terram te obtestor, ne feceris.   365

STRATOCLES
Hoc unum tibi negare cogor: caetera
Quae a me voles impetrare, feres ocyus.

EUBULUS
Quonam ibis? Sub quo duce facies stipendia?

STRATOCLES
Ibo in Pannoniam avibus quam faelicissimis,
Ibi occidam Turcarum multa millia.   370

EUBULUS
Satis Thrasonice.

EUBULUS

I am terrified: right now Mars is on your tongue, but after 350
combat ensues he will retreat to your feet, and instead of a
soldier, you will become a great deserter.[83]

STRATOCLES

Heaven forbid! Eubulus, don't speak that way. Much to
the contrary, gods willing, you will look upon (eventually) a
conqueror of many races, decorated with splendid spoils:[84] 355
Stratocles.

EUBULUS

More likely, I will see him laden with wounds and outrages.
But I beg you by your own head and whatever in this life is
most dear to you, look around you, and for just a moment of 360
time, consider a prudent course, my Stratocles. Don't brand
your parents with such great pain, for their comfort dies with
your parting. I pray by all the gods, I ask by heaven and earth, I 365
beseech you: do not do this.

STRATOCLES

I am forced to deny you this one thing. Anything else you
want to obtain from me, you will get more swiftly.

EUBULUS

Where in the world will you go? Under which general will
you perform your service?

STRATOCLES

I will go to Pannonia with the most favorable of omens,[85]
where I will kill many thousands of Turks.[86]   370

EUBULUS

Enough, Thraso.[87]

STRATOCLES

Nunc, quod reliquum est, vale,
Mi Praeceptor, mi custos, mi dulcis pater.
Nam si fuissem ex te natus, non potueras
Plus quam fecisti amore me amplexarier.
Multa in me constant fateor tua beneficia,   375
Quorum mihi memoriam nulla eripiet dies.
Quoad anima superabo mea, tui memor
Ero, mi Eubule: et te rogo quam maxime
Per bonitatem tuam, quam sensi crebrius,
Ut negligentiam meam atque ignaviam,   380
Omnesque culpas condones humaniter.

EUBULUS

Propemodum lacrymas tua verba excutiunt mihi,
Quando ingenuo ut adolescenti pulchrum est facis,
Agisque mihi tam liberales gratias.
Utinam hoc tuum exemplum sequantur caeteri: 385
Atque utinam in te merita mea augere liceat.
Quod quia non licet, age Stratocle, salve et vale:
Nam posthac utrum te visurus sim, ambigo.

STRATOCLES

Ego nihil ambigo.

EUBULUS

Deus te servet.

STRATOCLES

Vale. –

In hac turba sedere quosdam suspicor   A1.1
Quos magna super me teneat admiratio,
De improviso quid insanire coeperim,
Ut militatum vadam hiberno tempore,
Cum ver sive aestas sit longe opportunior.   A1.5

STRATOCLES

Now, as for the rest: goodbye, my teacher, my guardian, my
dear father. Even if I had been your son, you could not have
cherished me more lovingly than you have. I confess it, your 375
many kindnesses toward me are apparent, and no day will ever
snatch those memories from me. As long as I live and breathe,
I will remember you, my Eubulus, and I ask you, most especially
on account of your goodness, which I have often felt, to forgive 380
humanely my negligence, and my sloth, and all of my sins.[88]

EUBULUS

Your words almost provoke me to tears, since you are acting
as befits a young man of your status and you are expressing such
gentlemanly thanks to me.[89]

O if only the rest would follow this example of yours, and if 385
only it were possible to multiply my meritorious actions toward
you. Since that is not possible, Stratocles, go: goodbye and
farewell, for hereafter I doubt whether I will see you.

STRATOCLES

I don't doubt it at all.

EUBULUS

May God[90] protect you.

STRATOCLES

Farewell.
[*Exit Eubulus*]

1st addition[91]

I suspect that there are some people sitting in this crowd who A1.1
are greatly amazed at me. Why did I suddenly start to lose my
mind and enlist in the military during the wintertime, although A1.5
spring or summer is much more convenient? The answer to

Huic quaestioni facilis est responsio:
In hieme propter frigoris tyrannidem
Miles quiescit, et remissum agit otium,
Semper consuetum tollit sibi stipendium.
Altas ad urbes et opulentas ducitur.   A1.10
Illic est cornu copia rerum omnium,
Potestas fit cenare sumptuosius,
Vinumque bibere poculis maioribus,
Recubare in lectis placide usque in meridiem.
Istam volo primum militiam perdiscere,   A1.15
Quamvis eadem aliquantum iam usitata sit
Non mihi, sed vobis, qui potatis plusculum,
Et vosmet in cenam invitatis largius,
Tum dormiendo ceu glires pinguescitis.
E stativis placebit nonnunquam egredi,   A1.20
Gallinis tunc fiam vulpes, ovibus lupus,
Absque canibus venabor iucundissime.
Nam meus in praeda nasus est mere sagax
Odorator, subito si quid videt boni.

Ille hinc abiit: volo ego mecum hic meditarier   390
Accurate, quo pacto me in acie geram,
Etenim imparatum sese hostibus opponere,
Si recte cogito, praesens periculum est.
Ad hunc ergo modum volo ensem stringere,
Ita pedem laevum, sic firmabo dexterum,   395
Immobilis consistam ut instar Herculis.
Petitiones sic vero adversarias
Eludam. Ita hostes caesim summis viribus,
Lacertis retrorsum ductis rite feriam,
Eosdem punctim tali tetigero impetu,   400
Ensem per costas exigens saevissimum.
Multorum viscera hoc ferrum rimabitur,
Unde cerebrum fluet atro mistum sanguine.
Nonnullis digitos, aliis cervices metam,
Atque his ut caules detruncabo brachia.   405

this question is simple: in winter, on account of the tyranny of
the cold, a soldier relaxes, and enjoys his leave stress-free, and
keeps drawing his standard salary as usual. He goes to rich and A1.10
noble cities. There he sees a bountiful supply of everything;
there you have the right[92] to dine more lavishly and drink wine
from bigger goblets, and stay in bed peacefully clear into the
middle of the day. *This* is the military service I want to master A1.15
first. Now this kind of service is already somewhat customary--
not to *me*, but to all of you, who enjoy a glass now and again
[*Stratocles winks and nods*], and who generously invite yourselves
to dinner.[93] Then you sleep and get as fat as dormice.[94] Every so A1.20
often [*more winking and nodding*] we like to leave our quarters,[95]
and then I'll become a fox to the hens, a wolf to the sheep, and I
am very happy to go on the hunt without my pack of "hounds"[96]
[*more nudging and winking*]. For when it comes to booty, my
nose is a keen-scented purebred bloodhound,[97] as soon as it
picks up something good.[98]

   He is gone. Here by myself I wish to consider carefully how 390
I'll act in battle, since going to meet the enemy unprepared, if I
understand correctly, is surely an imminent danger. Therefore I
want to draw my sword like this, [*Draws sword dramatically*] and
plant my left foot like this and my right one like that, [*Assumes* 395
heroic stance] so I can stand immovable just like Hercules.[99] In
this way, I will definitely evade enemy attacks. Lifting my arms,
with a slash like this I will rightly strike down my foes with all
my might, and I'll also stab them with a thrust like that, driving 400
this most savage sword through their ribs. This blade will root
about[100] in the entrails of many, and where the brains flow out,
mixed with black blood.[101] I will sever the fingers and heads
from some, and hack off the arms from others, just as if they 405
were plant stalks.

Claudos efficiam caeso quosdam poplite.
Cadentum gemitus aurea tangent sidera.
Sed unum paene oblitus sum, quod maximum est,
Et quam quidvis aliud mage necessarium.
Quo pacto vortar in fugam? Sic, aestimo.   410
Parum scite curro: non est opus modo:
Quando erit opus, pedibus alas dabit timor.

STRATOCLES
Iam tandem dictis volo facere compendium: A2.1
Ego ut aspicitis hinc recta iam me confero
Ad militiam, pro Apolline Martem deligo,
Pro calamo gladium, pro atramento sanguinem.
Vos interibi transigite aevum ut vobis placet,   A2.5
Amplexi Musas suaviter osculamini
Omnes ad unam, virgines non virgines
Sed meretrices sunt omnium nequissimae,
Vestra exsorbentes raptim patrimonia.

Sed antequam urbe excedo, sodales mihi mei   413
Salutandi sunt, et complectendi ultimum.
Quid enim, si sese monitis impulsus meis
Addat socium unus, et alter ad rem bellicam,
Mecum ut facinora faciat immortalia?

FAUSTINA
Ego nunc, ego mulier omnium miserrima,   A3.1
Apud me sola conquerar vices meas;
Memet lugebo, quoniam qui me lugeat
Invenio praeter meipsam prorsus neminem.
O infaelix, o saeva, o intolerabilis   A3.5
Nuptarum conditio. O sors matrimonii,
Quam gravida es aerumnis aerumnosissimis
Et propemodum quotidianis mortibus!
Coniugium atque senectus videntur res duae
Persimiles: siquidem ambas adipisci omnes volunt,   A3.10

I will render some men lame by chopping their knees. The
groans of the fallen will reach the golden stars.[102]

But I have nearly forgotten one thing, which is the most
important, and more necessary than anything else. What will
I do if I am forced to flee? This is what I think I'll do. [*Shuffles* 410
and stumbles] I'm not an expert runner. I don't need to run right
now; when I do need to, fear will give wings to my feet.[103]

STRATOCLES [*Addresses the audience*]

Finally, now, I want to sum this up: As you see, I'm now going A2.1
straight from here into the service. I'm choosing Mars over
Apollo, the sword over the pen, blood over ink. You, meanwhile, A2.5
carry on your lives as you see fit: embrace and sweetly kiss all
the Muses one by one, those virgins who are not virgins but
whores, the most licentious of them all, who quickly suck dry
your inheritance. But before I leave the city, I must bid farewell 413
to my friends and embrace them one last time. But what if
someone else, spurred on by my advice, enlists for war with me,
so he too can perform immortal deeds?

[*Exit Stratocles*]

[*Enter Faustina*]

FAUSTINA

Now I, I the most miserable woman of them all, here by myself A3.1
all alone, I will lament my fate. I will mourn for myself, since
who would mourn me? I can find absolutely no one to mourn for
me besides myself. O, the ill-starred, cruel, unbearable condition A3.5
of wives! O, the lot of marriage, how pregnant you are with the
most distressing distresses and nearly daily deaths! Marriage
and old age seem to be two such similar things, inasmuch as all A3.10
people want to attain both, yet everyone complains when they

Accusant tamen omnes, ubi adepti sunt eas.
Neque id immerito: multo senes incommoda
Circumveniunt, et nos maritas excipit
Post gaudium breve longinquum infortunium.
Sed quas molestiarum moles senserim,   A3.15
Quaeque exantlarim totum per sexennium
Quo vir meus una fuit iisdem in penatibus,
Mitto dicere, quia meminisse horret animus.
Iam volvitur annus tertius, cum perditus
Ille, omnium terra quos haec sustinet   A3.20
Longe sceleratissimus, haud ullo numinis
Metu perstrictus, hominumve reverentia
Ulla tactus, me cum quaternis liberis
Illisque pusillis deseruit. Cor efferum,
Cor saxeum, et omni immanitate barbarum   A3.25
Orbatam me, atque a cognatis, affinibus,
Et amicis inopem, mulierem ante obitum suum
Fecit viduam: ipse, nescio qua mala cruce
Exagitatus, profugit hinc in Gallias,
In militiam scilicet, homo periurissimus,   A3.30
Et sacrilegissimus. Eheu, cur, qui temperas
Orbis totius solo nutu machinam,
Impune sinis tam horrendum patrari nefas?
Nec vero lamentarer hanc absentiam
Tantopere, si ad meque et communes liberos   A3.35
Alendos suppeditaret res quantum libet
Tenuis: nil aleator vinique barathrum
Fecit reliquum de patrimonio suo,
Quin etiam decoxit dotem meam ad obulum.
Post fabricando fabricam ferrariam   A3.40
Modico quaesticulo arcebat a nobis famem.
Nunc me extrema subegit egestas, semper aliquid
De ornamentis meis, deque suppellectili
Domestica divendere, ut sit quo mei
Vescantur in dies nati. quin aes quoque   A3.45

have obtained them.[104] And not undeservedly: ailments often
beset the elderly, and as for us brides, after a brief bit of joy a
long-lasting misfortune seizes us.

But what heaps of afflictions I felt, and what things I endured   A3.15
through the full six years my husband and I were together under
the same roof.[105] I avoid speaking of them, because my spirit
quails at the memory.[106] Now the third year has turned since
that depraved scoundrel—by far the most accursed of all those   A3.20
whom this earth sustains, a man virtually unrestrained by fear
of the divine, and untouched by any reverence for humanity —
deserted me along with these four children (and very young
at that). His heart, cruel, stony, and with every barbarous   A3.25
inhumanity, left me a woman bereft of relatives, neighbors, and
friends, and made a widow of his wife, even before his death.
He himself, driven on by some terrible unknown torment,[107]
ran away from here to Gaul, to military service evidently, a man   A3.30
treacherous and sacrilegious in the highest measure. Alas, you,
Jupiter, who control the workings of the whole universe with a
single nod,[108] why do you allow such a horrendous crime to be
committed with impunity?

To be sure, I would not lament his absence so very much, if   A3.35
there were some resources available, however slim, for supporting
me and our shared children. That dice player and bottomless pit
for wine left nothing from his inheritance, and he even distilled
my dowry down to the last penny. Later, by making money as   A3.40
a metalsmith, with this modest income he fended off famine
from us. Now extreme poverty has driven me to keep selling
off my jewelry and my household furnishings,[109] so there can be
something for my children to eat from day to day.   A3.45

Alienum contraxi, quod nisi dissolvero
Intra mensem alterum, impatiens me creditor
Aedibus evertet, ac fortunis omnibus.
Utinam vel ille redeat cito, vel mortuus
Mihi nuntietur, ut denuo possim viro   A3.50
Me iungere nuptiis. Nam quibus ego placeam,
Et qui thorum ambiant meum viri boni,
Honesti, locupletes haud desunt. Et licet
Quae sunt pudicae, non soleant nubere iterum,
Tamen si item faelices sint intellige,   A3.55
Quo nempe ad se tuendas nil egeant viris,
A me tot millibus abest sed faelicitas.
At enim si redeat vir meus, non faeminam
Effoeminatam, sed Leaenam aut Tygridem
Me reperiet. Et parum familiari modo   A3.60
Accipietur, uti posthac se teneat domi,
Bene educans quos seminavit liberos
Discatque me sibi uxorem non pellicem
Commissam esse a parentibus. Sic egero.

II.

TREMONIUS
Iu!

MISOMACHUS
    Iu!

TREMONIUS
        Salve, o patrium solum.

MISOMACHUS
            Salvete vos
Lares paterni, quos hoc per triennium
Non usurpavi luminibus, iamque eminus   420
Intueor, prae laetitia vix credens mihi.
Quot saeclis a vestro sinu procul abfui,

On top of all this, I have even gone into debt, and if I don't pay
it back within another month, my impatient creditor will turn
me out of my home—and out of all my fortune.[110]

If only he would either come back quickly, or be reported to   A3.50
me as dead, so that I could marry someone anew. For there are
those who find me attractive, and there is no shortage of good,
respectable, and wealthy men who are after[111] my marriage
bed.[112] And although there are some chaste women who are not
apt to marry a second time, still, if they are for their part happy,   A3.55
understand that it's presumably[113] because they have no need
of men to take care of them. That kind of happiness, however,
is very many miles away from me. But should my husband
return, he won't find a womanish woman, but rather a Lioness
or Tigress,[114] and I'll receive him in a manner insufficiently   A3.60
"familiar", so that hereafter he'll keep himself at home, properly
raising the children whom he sired,[115] and so that he'll learn
that I was entrusted to him by my parents as his *wife* and not
his mistress. *That's* what I'll do.

Act II

[*Enter Misomachus and Tremonius*]

TREMONIUS

Hooray!

MISOMACHUS

Hooray!

TREMONIUS

Hail, native soil. [*Kisses the ground*]

MISOMACHUS

I hail you, ancestral gods:[116] I have not laid eyes upon you for   420
these three years, and now I see you a mere spear's throw away;
I am so happy I can hardly believe it. How many ages have I

In extera regione, quo me insania,
Furorque vecors rapuit? Quare ut hoc meum
Ignoscatis peccatum, etiam atque etiam precor.   425
Si tale quidquam in posterum attentavero,
Dispeream exemplo pessimo.

TREMONIUS
                    Beatius
Haud aliquid omnes philosophastri finxerint,
Quam esse in tuto, longe a castris, longe ab acie,
Longe a vulneribus, longe ab Orci faucibus: 430
A quibus absunt profecto propius milites,
Quam navigantes, qui a morte digitis tribus
Duntaxat distant.

MISOMACHUS
                    Mars mors o vale, vale.
Abi Mars, nil tibi mecum rei est, abi, vale,
Te perdat ipse Iupiter, cruoris es   435
Nimium avidus, et homicida crudelissimus.

TREMONIUS
Praeclari bellatores fuimus.

MISOMACHUS
                    Maxume.
Quos cepimus, occidimus, et quos non cepimus,
Adhuc habemus.

TREMONIUS
                    Ha ha ha, pediculi,
Vestesque lacerae nostra sunt stipendia.   440
Moriar, si in sacculo habeo assem vel unicum.

MISOMACHUS
Curavi ego, ut mea praegnaret crumenula.

been away from your bosom, in a foreign land, where insanity and mad folly dragged me? And so I pray again and again that 425 you forgive my sin. Should I ever again hazard something like this in the future, may I die in the worst way.

TREMONIUS

All the foolosophers[117] have conceived of nothing more blessed than to be in one piece, far away from the camps, far away from the battlefield, far away from wounds, far away from 430 the jaws of death. Soldiers, to be sure, are not even as far from these as sailors, who are just three fingers from death.[118]

MISOMACHUS

Farewell, Mars! Farewell, death![119] Be gone, Mars! You have no business with me! Be gone! Farewell! May Jupiter himself 435 destroy you; you are too greedy for gore, and the cruelest killer.

TREMONIUS

Magnificent warriors is what we were.[120]

MISOMACHUS

The best. The ones we caught, we killed, and the ones we didn't catch, we still have.[121] [*Brushes lice from body*]

TREMONIUS

Ha, ha, ha - lice and tattered clothing are our pay. I'll die, if I 440 have even one penny in my pocket. [*Turns out empty pockets*]

MISOMACHUS

I made sure my pockets were bulging.

TREMONIUS
Curassem ego quoque, si furandi occasio
Oblata fuisset.

MISOMACHUS
        Quin tu linguam comprimis?
Nolo mihi mea strategemata memorarier.   445
Stolide nimirum fecimus, qui in tam grave,
Praesensque discrimen animas obtulerimus.

TREMONIUS
Tantosque labores hauserimus sine gloria.

MISOMACHUS
Nunc passim a notis conscindimur sibilis:
Ludus erimus apud cives, et iocus affatim.   450

TREMONIUS
Vah, melius opinor sibilari centies,
Quam iugulari semel. Vita nil carius.
Proin quantum dolebimus ludibrio,
Tantum laetemur nos vivere, et hoc amplius.
Pergamus porro.   455

MISOMACHUS
        Qui sunt, qui vestigia
Contra ponunt? Duo adolescentes scilicet.

TREMONIUS
Quasi in bellum profecturi, atque amentiae
Nostri futuri successores.

MISOMACHUS
        Alloquar.

TREMONIUS

I would have ensured the same thing, had the opportunity for stealing presented itself.

MISOMACHUS

Why don't you hold your tongue? I do *not* want to be reminded 445
of my exploits.[122] Without a doubt we acted stupidly when we offered up our lives to such a serious and present danger.

TREMONIUS

… And when we wasted so much effort without glory.

MISOMACHUS

Now everyone we know tears us to shreds and hisses at us.[123]
A laughing stock is what we'll be to our fellow citizens—and a 450
joke, really.[124]

TREMONIUS

Pfft, I suppose it's better to be hissed at a hundred times than to have your throat slit once. Nothing is more precious than life. So, the more we suffer from mockery, the happier we are to be alive, and then some. Let's keep going. 455

[*Enter Stratocles and Polemius*]

MISOMACHUS

Who are they? Who's coming our way? Two young men, no doubt.

TREMONIUS

As if setting off for war, and the successors-to-be of our madness.

MISOMACHUS

I'll talk to them.

III.

<small>Misomachus, Stratocles, Tremonius, Polemius.</small>

<small>Misomachus</small>
Heus iuvenes, sic, quae vultis, eveniant bona,
Quo tandem? Quo tenetis iter? At at scio   460
Iam qui sint.

<small>Stratocles</small>
        Et nos qui vos.

<small>Tremonius</small>
              Dii vostram fidem! Stratocles tu es,
et hic Polemius patruelis tuus.

<small>Polemius</small>
Et tu es Tremonius, miles nunc, olim aulicus.

<small>Stratocles</small>
Tu faber ille fabrorum alpha, et homo horarum omnium.

<small>Misomachus</small>
Iungamus dextras.   465

<small>Stratocles</small>
        Unde vos tam squalidi,
Pannosi, pulverulenti, ac sordibus obsiti?

<small>Tremonius</small>
Rogas? Inde, ubi vos duo perire statuitis.

Act III

Misomachus, Stratocles, Tremonius, Polemius

Misomachus
[*To Stratocles and Polemius*] Hey boys, I hope things are going well, but where are you going? [*To Tremonius*] But wait! *Now* I 460
know who they are.

Stratocles
And we know who you are.

Tremonius
For the love of god! You are Stratocles, and this is Polemius, your cousin.

Polemius
And you are Tremonius, now a soldier, once a courtier.

Stratocles
You are a craftsman, best of all craftsmen,[125] and a man for all seasons.[126]

Misomachus
Let's shake hands.   465
[*All shake hands*]

Stratocles
Where are you coming from, so dirty, ragged, dusty, and covered in filth?

Tremonius
You want to know? From the place where you two have decided to die.

POLEMIUS
Perire? non perire, pugnare volumus.
Facesse tu hinc cum dictis delirantibus.

STRATOCLES
Quin meliora ominare.   470

MISOMACHUS
                          Rem verbis tribus
Omnem effudit. Nulla est, nulla est bello salus.
Bellum est miseriarum pelagus altissimum:
Bellum malorum innumerorum compendium.

STRATOCLES
Ignavis atque imbellibus.

POLEMIUS
                          Ita suspicor,
Et vos esse credo fugitores acerrimos.   475
Strictorum aspectu concidistis ensium,
Fuerunt vobis in pedibus praecordia.
Premi potest vir fortis, sed non opprimi.

STRATOCLES
                                          Hem
Polemi, hoc verbum centum talentis emerim.

POLEMIUS
Inest in hoc corpore virtus, inest tibi   480
Testata magnis saepe rebus indoles.
Nos, quo invitat virtus, et immortalitas,
Eo divis faventibus concedimus.
Durum bellum? Dura pati praegestit animus.
Tecum, Stratocle, casus in omnes iverim: 485
Habeat nos socios mors eadem, aut victoria.

POLEMIUS

To die? Not to die, we wish to fight. Get out of here with
your crazy talk.

STRATOCLES

Come on, don't make such gloomy predictions.[127]   470

MISOMACHUS

In one breath he said the whole thing.[128] There is no, I repeat,
no, safety in war. War is the deepest sea of sorrows, and a
collection of countless evils.

STRATOCLES

For the cowards and wimps.

POLEMIUS

Here's what I think: that you two are the most decorated 475
deserters.[129] You keeled over at the sight of drawn swords, and
you put your hearts into fleeing on foot. A courageous man can
be hard-pressed, but not crushed.

STRATOCLES

Bravo, Polemius, I would buy those words for a million
dollars.

POLEMIUS

There is courage in this body of mine; in yours there are 480
natural qualities[130] often proven by great trials [*Indicates
Stratocles*]. Where virtue and immortality call us - *that's* where
we're going, God willing. War is cruel? My spirit is ready and
willing to suffer cruelties. With you, Stratocles, I would march 485
toward any end. Let us be comrades, together either in death or
in victory!

TREMONIUS
Qui sapiunt, illi ex alienis incommodis
Sua norunt pulchre praecavere incommoda.
Sunt multa, quae nunquam cuiquam experiunda sunt:
In his qui bellum numerat, non male numerat.   490

MISOMACHUS
In pace clarum fieri non minus licet
Quam in bello.

STRATOCLES
                    Scimus hoc.

MISOMACHUS
                                At illa neutiquam
Scitis, quae nos perpetiendo cognovimus.

POLEMIUS
Narrate, dabimus operam.

TREMONIUS
                                Nox citius diem
Abstulerit, si memorare velimus singula.   495
Atque illud primum esto: tales redibitis,
Quales videtis nos. Hui, contemplamini
Utriusque cultum, ut placet?

STRATOCLES
                                Apage cum ista tua
Praedictione: avis sinistra es, nihil agis.

POLEMIUS
Ad Persas et Turcas cum istoc vaticinio.   500
Torquati, et annulati, et operti purpura
Cum diis volentibus in patriam redibimus.

MISOMACHUS
O adolescens, tui te fallent spiritus,

TREMONIUS

Sensible people have learned from another's calamities to guard carefully against their own catastrophes.[131] There are many things that no one should ever experience. Whoever 490 counts war among these, does not count wrongly.

MISOMACHUS

It is no less likely to become famous in peace than in war.[132]

STRATOCLES

We know this.

MISOMACHUS

Yes, but neither of you has any idea about all the things we learned through raw experience.

POLEMIUS

Enlighten us; we'll pay attention.

TREMONIUS

Night would sooner steal away the day,[133] if we wanted to 495 recall events one by one. But let this be the first point: you will return in the same state you now see us. So, look at our clothing, do you like it?

STRATOCLES

Get out of here with your lousy prediction.[134] You are a bad omen and good for nothing.

POLEMIUS

To the Persians and Turks with that prophecy.[135] With the 500 gods' blessing, we will return to our fatherland adorned with torques and rings, and swathed in purple.[136]

MISOMACHUS

O young man, your bravery will betray you, and it will give

Dabuntque malum tibi, tuisque gravissimum.
Quae gloria bello capitur victis hostibus,   505
Ea penes imperatorem, non militem
Est: ille felix, ille victor dicitur:
Illius est triumphus, praeda illius est,
Illius sunt captivi: nostrae vigiliae,
Humicubationes, non in lectulis,   510
Crebra itinera, frigus, aestus, esuries, sitis,
Vulnera demum, et caedes.

TREMONIUS
                              Et his plura insuper:
Nec ullae aliquando referri gratiae solent.
Canibus, equis, asinis utuntur mitius,
Quam nobis, quos tanquam pilas habent, et huc   515
Et illuc iactant longe importunissime.
Si declinaris a praescripto paululum,
Neque id consulto, sed per imprudentiam,
Indicta caussa mox suspendunt arbori,
Quamvis dives, formosus sis, ac nobilis,   520
Quamvis per omnia sacra lacrymans obsecres.

MISOMACHUS
Sexcentos vidi raptari ad suspendium,
Aetate, et forma iuvenes florentissimos,
Vobis aequales, quorum nos valde miseret.
Quin mihi bis terve iniecta iam restis fuit,   525
Cum me lethali vivum de periculo
Divina sors quaedam servavit. Hanc sibi
Sperantem adire discrimina, non mentis est
Sanae. Quando visum est superis, ferunt opem,
Non quando homines eorum auxilia postulant.   530

you and yours the gravest misfortunes.

Whatever glory is taken from conquered enemies in war 505
becomes the commander's possession, not the soldiers'. *He* is
declared fortunate, *he* is declared victor: *his* is the triumph, *his*
are the spoils, *his* are the captives. Ours is the midnight watch,
the lying on the ground (not in beds), the frequent marches, the 510
bitter cold, the burning heat, the hunger, the thirst, then at last
the wounds and slaughter.

TREMONIUS

And there are even more in addition to these. Thanks are
never given...ever. Dogs, horses, and asses are used more gently
than we are. They use *us* like playthings, throwing us ruthlessly 515
here and there, far and wide. If you deviate from a direct order
even a little - not even intentionally, but through ignorance
- without a trial, they hang you from a tree, no matter how 520
wealthy, handsome, or noble you are, no matter how much you
tearfully beg by all things sacred.

MISOMACHUS

I saw six hundred[137] men dragged off to be hanged, young
men in the full bloom of their youth and beauty, similar to you,
and we greatly pitied them. In fact, I've had a noose put on 525
me two or three times now, but some divine fate saved my life
from mortal peril. To approach dangers while hoping for some
miracle like this is insane.[138] The gods above bring aid only
when they see fit, not when men pray for their assistance. 530

STRATOCLES
Memini hoc ipso die a docto quodam viro
Similia multa audire, et exponi mihi
Ad terrorem incutiendum copiosius,
Quibus scateat bellum calamitatibus: et haec
Oratio vestra, ut oculatorum testium,   535
Quorum vel unus superat auritos decem,
Animum meum labascentem aliquantum impulit.

POLEMIUS
Quid hoc, Stratocle? Siccine leves ratiunculae
Argumenta tibi videntur firmissima?
Tolle moras, fiat quod coeptum est viriliter.   540

STRATOCLES
Non haec tantum, nec illa tantum me movent,
Verum utraque, Polemi, quando simul pondero.
Nunc demum intelligo, quam sapienter meus
Magister mihi castra, et bellum disuaserit.
Caecus qui eram, nunc dispicio clarissime.   545

POLEMIUS
Rem portentosam: hic vir erat, nunc est foemina:
Arma fremebat, calathos et lanam cogitat.
Quod male amicum numen vos adduxit hodie?
Qui ex re confecta facitis infectissimam,
Sermonibus istis multo mendacissimis.   550
Agite negotium vestrum, sinite via
Quam ingredimur nos proficisci recta ad Hungaros:
Nam vos e Belgica, ut reor, repedastis huc.

TREMONIUS
Idem Mars hic, idem Mars ibi, eadem mala
Bellum bellantibus affert ubivis gentium.   555
Et nos animo bono, ac vestri cupidissimo
Conamur vos abducere ab hac sententia,
Quae de mansuetis reddit rabiosissimos,
Ex ovibus pardos, et leones, et lupos:
Haec monstra rapto vivunt atque sanguine   560
Aliarum animantium, quod faciunt milites.

STRATOCLES

I remember hearing many similar things on this very day
from a certain learned man. He told me at great length about
the abundant calamities of war to strike fear into me. And this
speech of yours, like the speech of eyewitnesses, even one of 535
which surpasses ten ear-witnesses,[139] compels my courage to
quiver a little.

POLEMIUS

What is *this*, Stratocles? Do these flimsy accounts seem like
solid arguments to you? Away with delay! What we began as 540
men, let us finish as men.

STRATOCLES

Neither one set of arguments alone, nor just the other move
me, but both, Polemius, when I weigh them together. Now at
last I realize how wise my teacher was to dissuade me from
military life and war. I, who was blind, now see most clearly.   545

POLEMIUS

How monstrous! This was a man, but now is a woman [*Indicates
Stratocles*]. He was raging for weapons, now he's thinking of
flower baskets and fleece.[140] What evil god has brought you two
here today? You are undoing a done deal with your incredibly 550
deceitful words. Go mind your own business, get out of our way
and let us[141] march straight for the Hungarians:[142] for, as I see,
you have just retraced your steps back here from Belgium.

TREMONIUS

The same Mars here, the same Mars there,[143] the same evils
brought by battle to all those waging war anywhere in the 555
world. And we are trying with the best intentions (and in your
interest) to turn you away from this plan, which changes the
tame into the rabid, sheep into leopards and lions and wolves.
These monsters live off of their prey and the blood of other 560
living creatures, which is what soldiers do.

MISOMACHUS
Geratur bellum ab iis, defendendi sui
Quos compellit necessitas, hi mutuo
Sese discerpant, dilanient, ferro necent.
Quis hic furor, atram bello mortem accersere?   565
Imminet, ac per se tacitis venit ipsa pedibus.
Quod fatum est, tantis vos ingeniis praeditos,
Tam illustrium hominum filios, tam divites,
Aetate tam virenti in media arma ruere,
Nulla laesos iniuria? Dum tempus est,   570
Consilia, obtestor, saniora capessite.
A nobis mutuam sumite prudentiam,
Si ipsi caretis: temeritas saepe nocuit.

TREMONIUS
Redite, redite ad intermissam Palladem:
Ego rediturus servitutem ad aulicam,   575
Ad incudem hic et malleum se recipiet,
Desertam ad uxorem, et desertos liberos.
Cui dulce est praelium, nec pueri instar sapit.

STRATOCLES
Quid adhaec, Polemius?

POLEMIUS
                           Eundem est, surdo fabula
Canitur.   580

STRATOCLES
          O qui secutus es me devium,
Sequere in viam redeuntem.

MISOMACHUS
                          Ne quid haesita,
Largire vitam annosque tuos patriae magis,
Quam incognitis, de te qui meruerunt nihil.

MISOMACHUS

Let war be waged by those forced by necessity to defend themselves; let *them* mutilate each other, tear each other into pieces, and kill each other with swords. What kind of madness 565 is this, to summon war's mournful death?[144] It is stalking[145] us and coming by itself, of its own accord, with silent steps. What is your fate? You are gifted with so much natural ability, the sons of such brilliant men, so wealthy, in the prime of life. Will you charge into the thick of battle even though you've suffered 570 no insult? While there is time, I implore you, pursue a safer course.[146] Borrow prudence from us if you have none yourselves: rashness is often harmful.

TREMONIUS

Go back, go back to your interrupted studies:[147] I am going 575 back to serve the court; he will go back to his anvil and hammer, to his deserted wife and deserted children. Whoever likes battle has less sense than a child.[148]

STRATOCLES

What about this, Polemius?

POLEMIUS

We need to go; this story falls on deaf ears.[149]   580

STRATOCLES

O Polemius, you who followed me down the crooked path, follow me as I return to the straight and narrow.

MISOMACHUS

Don't hesitate at all to give your life and years bountifully to your fatherland rather than to those you don't know, who deserve nothing from you.

TREMONIUS
Gaudebis semper, si hos monitus audiveris.
Si proieceris, aeternum te poenituerit.   585

POLEMIUS
Volenti nolenti persuadetis mihi.
Quoniam igitur vobis videtur omnibus,
Mihi literas, et me restituam literis.

STRATOCLES
Factum optime. Vos sequimini, ut labore pro
Vestro detur vobis coena extructissima.   590

TREMONIUS
Bene profecto: etenim iam diebus plus decem
Incoenatus durat uterque.

MISOMACHUS
                          Ego visam prius
Uxorem, tum ad vos accedam.

STRATOCLES
                          Pietas iubet.

MISOMACHUS
In vita nihil unquam adeo optatum contigit,
Nihil aeque faustum, laetum, et gaudii plenum,   595
Meae uxori ut hodie mea haec reversio
Continget improvisa: de collo meo
Pendebit, os et lacrymis opplebit sibi.
Accurret ad genua mea dehinc pusillus grex
Natorum ingeminantum pater, pater, pater.   600
Ipse quoque mihi iterum natus videbor, et
Complexuum, osculorumque haud satias erit.

TREMONIUS

You'll always be glad if you heed these warnings. If you reject 585
them, you'll regret it for eternity.

POLEMIUS

Whether I want it or not, you are convincing me. So, since it
seems right to all of you, I will restore my studies to myself and
myself to my studies.

STRATOCLES

Well done. Everyone follow me, so that in return for your
trouble you'll get an extravagant feast.   590

TREMONIUS

Excellent idea! For more than ten days now both of us have
gone dinner-less.
[*Indicates Misomachus*]

MISOMACHUS

I'll see my wife first, then I'll join you.

STRATOCLES

Responsibility demands it.[150]

MISOMACHUS

It turns out that nothing in life is desired so much, nothing 595
is so auspicious, so happy and so full of joy, as this unexpected
return of mine today for my wife.[151] She will hang from my
neck, and tears will flow down her face. And then my tiny
flock of children will run to my knees crying 'Father, Father, 600
Father,' and I will seem to myself reborn, and there will hardly
be enough hugs andkisses.

[*Enter Faustina*]

MISOMACHUS
… [Complectendo osculandoque satiarier   A.4.1-2
Non potero.] Eccam domo prodit coniux mea.
O mea Faustina, faustitas mea, mel meum,
Mea anaticula, mea animula et Iuno mea:
Siquidem ego tibi nunc revenio magnus Iupiter.   A.4.5
Valen', valuistin'? Da complexum et suavium.

FAUSTINA
Quis tu qui tam impudenter me affari audeas
Et amplexum petere? In malam rem, furcifer.

MISOMACHUS
Eho! Iocone istuc an serio?

FAUSTINA
                  Quid? An
Tu te meum maritum praedicas?   A4.10

MISOMACHUS
                    Ego
Sum.

FAUSTINA
  Non es!

MISOMACHUS
         Certe sum.

FAUSTINA
              Non es.

MISOMACHUS
                Quis ergo sum,
Si non sum is qui sum?

FAUSTINA
              Homo nequam es atque perfidus
Nullius pretii, scelerum egregius artifex.

MISOMACHUS [*Addresses the audience*]

    [Hugs and kisses won't satisfy me.][152]   A4.1-2

    Look, here comes my wife out of the house. O my Faustina, my fabulous fortune,[153] my honey, my little duckling, my soul, and my Juno (since I, as great Jupiter,[154] am now returning to A4.5 you). How are you, how have you been? Give me a hug and a kiss.

FAUSTINA

    Who are you to address me so brazenly and ask for a hug? Go to hell, you bastard.[155]

MISOMACHUS

    Whoa! Is this a joke, or are you serious?

FAUSTINA

                           What?

    Are you claiming to be my husband?   A4.10

MISOMACHUS

    I am.

FAUSTINA

    You are not!

MISOMACHUS

    Of course I am.

FAUSTINA

    You are not.

MISOMACHUS

    Who then am I, if I am not who I am?

FAUSTINA

    A worthless, lying, good-for-nothing man, a notorious craftsman of crimes.

MISOMACHUS
Ebriane es an sobria? Quae contumeliis
Tuum virum sic proscindas? Nisi plurimum   A.4.15
Ac plus oculis te amarem, iam caput tibi
Pugnis mulcerem.

FAUSTINA
                    Tu ut me pulses insuper?
Sceleste, vapula!

MISOMACHUS
                    Au, au, ah, ah quid facis?

FAUSTINA
Num in concubinatum me tibi credis datam,
Quam possis ludere quomodo et quoties velis?   A4.20
Comedisti rem patriam, dotem meam
Per luxuriam absumpsisti, me in summa inopia
Cum parvis liberis omni solatio
Spoliatam destituisti, et quantum in te fuit
Nos ad mendicitatem trusisti improbe.   A.4.25
Non te agnosco, discede hinc, repete Gallias,
Ibi volutare cum scortis venalibus.
Non me tractasti ut coniugem: nec te ut virum
Tractabo, fac me missam.

MISOMACHUS
                    Iracunda es nimis.
An ego primus, ab uxore qui recesserit?   A4.30
Factum est hoc alias et fiet adhuc saepius.
Neque tamen ulla redeuntem ad se virum
Repulit, nec verbis tam insurrexit asperis,
Nedum ut misellum fustibus dolaverit
Ut tu.   A4.35

FAUSTINA
          Nondum quae facta sint omnia tenes.

MISOMACHUS

Are you drunk or sober? Who are you to lash your man like this with insults? If I didn't love you more than anything and A4.15 even more than my eyes,[156] right now I would caress your head with these fists.

FAUSTINA

So you would beat me on top of all this? Take that [*strikes him*], you criminal!

MISOMACHUS

Ow, ow, ah, ah, what are you doing?

FAUSTINA

So, do you think that I was given to you as a mistress and not as a wife, someone you can fool around with however and how A4.20 often you want? You ate up your father's estate; you squandered my dowry through your extravagance; you left me with small children, completely destitute, stripped of all solace, and as far as you could you drove us disgracefully into beggary. I do not A4.25 recognize you[157] as my own: get out of here, go back to your Gaul, where you wallow with your cheap whores. You did not handle me as a wife; nor will I handle you as a husband. Let me go.

[*Attempts to get free of Misomachus, who is trying to hold on to her*].

MISOMACHUS

You get angry too easily. Am I the first man to part from his A4.30 wife? It has happened before and it will happen yet again. Even so, no woman has rejected her husband upon his return, nor revolted with such harsh words, much less rained blows on the poor man, as you have. A4.35

FAUSTINA

You don't yet know everything that's happened.

MISOMACHUS
Eia ignosce.

FAUSTINA
            Cave ad me propius accesseris.

MISOMACHUS
Abibo, et aliam uxorem reperiam mihi.

FAUSTINA
Insania ipsa insanior erit, quae tibi
Nupserit, ita nec unum pilum viri boni
Habes.   A4.40

MISOMACHUS
            Faustina, mitte maleloqui, et cito
Iniuriarum oblita funditus domum
Me admitte, mihique tribue honorem pristinum,
Mementoque dominum me tibi, non servulum
Esse adiunctum a supremo Rege coelitum.
Aut istum ensem defigam in corpore tuo   A4.45
Usque ad capulum et hic sanguinem tuum canes
Delingent.

FAUSTINA
            Siccine pruriunt scapulae tibi?
Accipe.

MISOMACHUS
            Satis est, satis est, cessa, cessa obsecro. –
Scelestiorem, audaciorem, et impiam
Magis et furentem me vidisse faeminam   A4.50
Non puto. Quam blande coniugalemque in modum
Est me amplexata! Quam osculata suaviter!
Tanquam suem a foribus propulit atrociter.
Credebam me duxisse agnam placidissimam,
Duxi pestiferam belluam. Quo nunc eam?   A4.55

MISOMACHUS
    Come on, let it go.

FAUSTINA
    Watch out; don't come any closer to me.

MISOMACHUS
    Fine, I'll go away and find myself another wife.

FAUSTINA
    Whoever marries you will be crazier than craziness itself;
    every single hair on your head is worthless.[158]   A4.40

MISOMACHUS
    Faustina, enough with the abuse, forget these wrongs, all
    of them completely, and quickly let me come back home, and
    bestow upon me again my former position, and remember that
    I was joined to you by the highest King of heaven as your *master*,
    not your slave. Either that, or I will thrust this sword into your A4.45
    body all the way to the hilt and on this spot the dogs will lick
    up your blood.

FAUSTINA [*Strikes him repeatedly*]:
    So, are your shoulders sore now? Take that!

MISOMACHUS
    That's enough, that's enough, stop, stop, I beg you.

    [*Exit Faustina*]

    I don't think I've ever seen a more wicked, uppity, impious,
    and raving woman. How gently and just like a wife she   A4.50
    embraced me! How sweetly she kissed me! She savagely drove
    me outside as if I were a pig. I used to believe that I had married
    the gentlest of lambs, but I married a pernicious beast. Where
    will I go now?   A4.55

Quo me vertam? Ad bellum redire tam lubet
Quam ad inferos. Alibi nemo mortalium
Me novit, in hac urbe manere mihi non licet
Absque probro ingenti. Omnes credunt adulterum
Me factum, quoniam me uxor sic excluserit.   A4.60
Ridebor etiam qui sim passus verbera
A muliere, quam me verberare oportuit
Naturae legibus, quas fregi turpiter.
Nae miser est qui caret uxore, ille miserior
Qui quam est nactus bonam et probam, amittit brevi,   A4.65
Ille est miserrimus, qui pessimam diu
Retinere cogitur, quia mors non vult gradum
Accelerare, ut det finem calamitatibus.
Quod mihi ne eveniat maximum est periculum,
Quando uxor mea iam coepit quarta esse furia.   A4.70
Mulierum natura impatiens libidinis
Consuevit esse; quid si dum in castris ego
Operam do Marti, illa suum sibi Martem quoque
Invenerit, cui det operam? Atque haec causa sit,
Quid illa me tectis prohibeat? Ultimum   A4.75
Isti castello expugnando applicabimus
Arietem; parva saepe mora iras fervidas
Et implacabiles domuit.

                        Exit foras
Sine baculo: bene est, verba ego malo mala,
Quam plagas. Faustina, mea lux meaque salus,   A4.80
Ah, multum offendi, qui te mulierem optimam
Et qua sol meliorem in terris nusquam aspicit,
Pulcherrimam, castissimam, fidissimam,
Tuosque meosque liberos foedifragus
Deserui in re angusta. Pro quo poenam mihi   A4.85
Quamcumque tu irrogaveris, feram libens,
Tantum mecum ut redeas veterem in concordiam,
Meque ad te recipias.

FAUSTINA
                        Num te ergo paenitet
tui flagitii ex intimo pectore?

Where shall I turn? Returning to war is as appealing as going
to hell. In any other place no man alive knows me, but I can't
stay in this city without disgrace. Everyone believes I've become
an adulterer because my wife has shut me out like this. I'll be   A4.60
a laughingstock, since I've suffered a beating from a woman, a
woman it was *my* right to beat, according to the laws of nature,
which I've shamefully broken.

Alas, wretched is the man who has no wife; more wretched
is the one who has taken a good and upstanding wife and lost   A4.65
her within a short time; but most wretched is the man forced
to keep a terrible wife for a long time, because death does not
wish to quicken its step and thereby end his suffering.[159] The
danger of this happening to me is very great, since my wife has   A4.70
just become the fourth Fury.[160]

Women are by nature unable to control their lust:[161] what if
while I am in camp paying attention to Mars, she also finds
herself her own Mars, to whom she can "pay attention"?[162] And
what if this is the reason why she's keeping me from the house?   A4.75
Finally, to take this stronghold by storm, I'll bring to bear the
battering ram;[163] often a slight delay has mastered raging and
implacable anger.[164]

[*Enter Faustina*]

She's coming outside without a stick. That's good, since I
prefer insults to injuries. Faustina, my light and salvation,[165]   A4.80
ah, I have offended you deeply. You are the best of women; in
all the world the sun has never shone upon a better one. You
are the most beautiful, the most chaste, the most faithful, yet I
treacherously[166] deserted you and the children, yours and mine,
in dire straits. For this I'll willingly bear whatever punishment   A4.85
you inflict, so long as you return with me to our former harmony,
and take me back to you.

FAUSTINA

Do you therefore repent for your sin with all your heart?[167]

MISOMACHUS
                        Deum
Testem appello, paenitet ex pectore intimo.   A4.90

FAUSTINA
Non es facturus amplius?

MISOMACHUS
                                Non amplius.
Iuro terram, iuro mare, iuro sidera:
Si fecero, dii mihi faciant magnum malum.

FAUSTINA
Potatione et lusu temperabis?

MISOMACHUS
                        Ach
Ne dubites, temperabitur.   A4.95

FAUSTINA
                                Et fidem coles
Maritalem?

MISOMACHUS
                Etiam, ad extremum usque spiritum.

FAUSTINA
Et exercebis quam didicisti fabricam?
Ut sit quod nos edamus?

MISOMACHUS
                                Exercebitur.
Quid multis opus est? In tuo sum arbitrio.

FAUSTINA
Nunc intra!   A4.100

MISOMACHUS
                Uxorem possideo plane auream!
Iu! iu! iu!

MISOMACHUS
    I call God[168] as my witness; I repent with all my heart.   A4.90

FAUSTINA
    You won't do it anymore?

MISOMACHUS
    No more. I swear by the earth, I swear by the sea, I swear by
the stars: If I do, may the gods bring me great evil.

FAUSTINA
    You will limit the drinking and dice?

MISOMACHUS
    Oh,[169] don't worry, they'll be limited.   A4.95

FAUSTINA
    And you will honor marital fidelity?[170]

MISOMACHUS
    Indeed, until my last breath.

FAUSTINA
    And you will practice the trade you learned? So there will be
something for us to eat?

MISOMACHUS
    I will. What more do you want? I am under your control.[171]

FAUSTINA
    Now come in! [*Faustina flings open door, and arms*]   A4.100

MISOMACHUS
    I have a wife of gold! Hooray! Hooray! Hooray!

Endnotes

1. 1-100: This lengthy opening tirade against school life is similar in both invective tone and in some individual arguments to Seneca, *Letters* (= *Ep.*) 88.

2. 3 **maleficos**, "criminals": The related noun **maleficium**, "evil deed," was originally a neutral term, but from the time of Tacitus (1st - 2nd century CE) the word was associated with malign magic and sorcery. In the sixteenth century **maleficus** became a synonym for black magician. The individuals who performed witchcraft were termed **malefici** and were men and women of lower social class with little education who were different only in their perceptions of magical power and malevolence (Broedel 131-136).

    In Dillingen "the foundation of the University of Dillingen, which was placed under Jesuit control in 1563, made the Bishopric [of Augsburg] a 'citadel of German Catholicism', with an enormous influence in the region" (Behringer 123). The witch hunts and trials in the city were very influential and cited as models in courts in Munich and at the University of Ingolstadt from 1587 into the late 1620s. Their influence was also seen in smaller territories both Catholic and Protestant (Behringer 123). Students would likely have been present at the questioning and torturing of suspected witches at this time, and would have seen some of the implements mentioned in line 5. This makes Stratocles' claims that student life is worse than torture appear exaggerated. On the other hand, flogging was common, and first year students especially had to undergo institutionally approved and administered hazing that included harsh physical treatment; cf. Pontanus' *Progymnasma* 84 and our appendix on Renaissance Hazing.

3. 6 **Phalaridis, aut Mezentii**, "Phalaris or Mezentius": Phalaris and Mezentius were two literary "tyrants" whose names were proverbial for cruelty. Phalaris used to put his victims into a bronze replica of a bull and then put a fire under it; the screams of the roasted victims would produce the "roar" of the bull; cf. Cicero, *Against Verres* (=*Ver.*) 4.73 and Diodorus Siculus 9.19.1. Mezentius, an enemy of Aeneas in Vergil's *Aeneid*, was an atheist and notoriously brutal. He would tie live victims face-to-face

to corpses and leave the bound couple out in the sun (*Aen.* 8.483-488). Erasmus frequently made reference to these two tyrants in his writings, always referring to their extraordinary cruelty: *Collected Works*, Vol. 9, *"Correspondence,"* p. 366; *Education of a Christian Prince*, pp. 25-26; *Complaint of Peace*, p. 32; Drummond, p. 104.

4. 15 **fullo**, "fuller": In Classical times a fuller cleaned cloth, often ceremonial togas, by bleaching them with urine and sulphur and sometimes whitening them with chalk. In Pontanus' time the fuller performed similar tasks, removing dirt, oils, and other impurities and thickening the cloth. The next step was tenting, which involved stretching the cloth on large frames. It was also a term used for those who made cloth. "Dry cleaner" is a reasonable modern equivalent.

5. 16 **Nobis ... non licet**, "But we students ... death": This is perhaps a reworking for the context of a more general notion expressed in similar words in Ovid's *Metamorphoses* 3.153-154: (everyone must die, so) **dicique beatus / ante obitum nemo supremaque funera debet**, "no one should be called blessed before his death and last funeral rites".

6. 20 **noverca**, "stepmother": Stepmothers were proverbially evil in Latin literature, in epic and tragedy as well as in comedy and later comic prose. A possible parallel would be the "annoying mother-in-law" of contemporary comedy, but ancient stepmothers were worse: they were feared for being willing to commit murder in order to give preference (and a better chance at inheritance) to their own children. Medea was the chief example, and is referred to as **saeva noverca**, "savage mother-in-law" in Ovid (*Heroides* 6.126-128) and Vergil (*Georgics* 2.128), two authors Pontanus knew intimately and wrote about extensively. A more contemporary reference to harsh stepmothers occurs in Erasmus' works, which Pontanus knew just as intimately. A famous proverb by Erasmus reads, **Ipsa dies quandoque, parens quandoque noverca** "The same day is at one time a mother, at another a stepmother" (*Adagia* 764 = I.8.64). Also in *Dulce Bellum Inexpertis* "War is sweet to those without experience of it," Erasmus discusses what Mother Nature would say if she witnessed the men she created going to war with one another. He conjectures that Nature, enraged, would call out, "What hell has produced this monstrosity [war] for us? There are some who call me a harsh stepmother because in the whole grand total of things I made...a few animals that were not gentle--although no beast is so savage that it cannot be tamed by skill and kindness...Who then is this, worse than a stepmother, who has given us this new beast, a plague to all the world?" (Erasmus, *Adages*, IV.i.1, *Collected Works*, vol. 35, pp. 406-407).

7. 21 **sexcentos**, "six hundred": Six hundred is used here as a metaphor for "uncountable/innumerable years", as perhaps in Plautus *Trinummus* 791

sescentae ad eam rem causae possunt conligi "six hundred reasons can be attached to this matter." Cf. a similar use in 522 below.

8. 23 **quindecim**, "fifteen": Cf. line 59, where he asks the audience to count up whether he has correctly enumerated his years of study. The Jesuit Curriculum consisted of courses in a sequential order of Humanities, Philosophy, and Theology, the duration of which totaled 14 years. The Humanistic Curriculum incorporated three years of grammar followed by one year each in humanities and rhetoric. Since the student in our play refers to philosophy classes as the last attended, we can ignore the years of theology that would follow. So, when he says he did Philosophy at least 6 years, he did it twice. He further admits to having done Rhetoric for 4 years (i.e., 4 times). That makes 10. Let us now assume he did Grammar (3) and Humanities (1) without repetition, and we arrive at 14. This proves the point that he is not good at adding numbers, and justifies his challenge ("do the math" line 59). Another (remote) possibility is that he alludes here to the ancient Roman custom of counting "inclusively", i.e., without a real zero. On that system the 14 years just described would add up to 15. There is no clear reference to this, however, and elsewhere Stratocles seems to be a less than exemplary student. It thus seems best to take this discrepancy in numbers as a joke at his expense. For further detail see Pavur; Padberg.

9. 29 *c'est moi*, "it's me": We render the Greek words that appear in the text, οὗτος ἐκεῖνος, as a French phrase. This is probably a reference to Aristotle's theory of communication. In his *Poetics* 1448b16-17 and in his *Rhetoric* 1371b9 he states that recognizing someone or identifying an image with its original ("Oh, this is him!") is a source of pleasure. Cf. Sifakis 43-52 and 152 f..

10. 29 **trivi asserem**, "wore ... bench": This is our attempt to make vivid the more literal "how strongly I wore out/away the wooden beam," which in English is pretty dull.

11. 30 **Orbilius ... plagosus**, "Orbilius ... flogging": Cf. Horace, *Epistles* 2.1.70-71 **... memini quae plagosum mihi parvo / Orbilium dictare** "I remember what Orbilius the flogger (full of floggings) used to say to me when I was little". Orbilius is the classical name for a schoolmaster in humanistic drama. Flogging was part of student life. Pontanus wrote a few pieces on flogging in his *Progymnasmata*, his "preliminary or warm-up exercises" for learning Latin (e.g., **De plagis,** "On Flogging") and in some of his university speeches (**Disputationes**), e.g. "Whether young boys should be punished with blows" (see Leinsle 2005, 91). See notes below on 33 **corpusculum** and 36, and the appendix on Hazing.

12. 33 **corpusculum**, "poor bodies": We make a generalizing plural out of

a generalizing singular in the Latin. Cf. Erasmus, *Colloquia* (in *Opera Omnia*, ord. 1, tom. 3), "Militis et Cartusiani", line 83: ... **quibus rebus corpusculum alatur** ..., translated by Thompson (*Collected Works* 39, p. 332, line 36) as: " ... how this poor body is nourished ..." Cf. also *Ratio studiorum* § 363 (translation Pavur), from the Rules Common to Professors of the Lower Classes: "Nothing preserves the entire effort of well-ordered learning as effectively as the observance of the rules. ... This will be achieved more easily by the hope of honor and award and by the fear of shame than it will be by corporal punishment."

13. 36 **Grammaticam ... poetica,** "What then ... poetry": Stratocles implies that flogging was part of the fundamentals, the "grammar" of his early "grammar" schooling, and that having "mastered" that he moves on to other subjects.

14. 38 **Musas,** "Muses": Nine daughters of Zeus and Mnesmosyne, a personification of memory. They are hailed by ancient sources as the goddesses of inspiration in the humanities and intellectual creativity. The invocation of the muses is common at the beginning of works by ancient poets such as Hesiod, Homer, and Virgil. See below on 46 **Calliope**. For more detail see Harris and Platzner 67-69.

15. 46 **Domina Calliope,** "Lady Calliope": Muse of Epic Poetry invoked by epic poets. According to Hesiod (*Theog.* 78-100), Calliope is foremost among the Muses, for it is through her blessing that a man is able to use words to distinguish himself from his fellow men.

16. 47 **Linumque, Rhesumque,** "Linus and Rhesus": Linus was son of Apollo and a muse (Urania or Calliope or some other); on Rhesus cf. Cicero, *On the Nature of the Gods* (= *ND*) 3.18.45 **et Orpheus et Rhesus di sunt Musa nati** "Both Orpheus and Rhesus are gods born from a Muse." This is a reference to a theological question debated in Pontanus' time: can a woman who has given birth (i.e, Mary to Jesus) remain a virgin? Ignatius of Loyola raises the question in his *Autobiography* (ch. 15), where he converses with a Moor who cannot be persuaded that a woman could give birth to a child and remain a virgin. Thomas Aquinas had maintained (*Summa Theologica* III. 28, disp. 4, art. 3 c) that Mary remained a virgin after having given birth to Jesus. One problem was whether she had a sexual relationship with Joseph and possibly children with him. His answer insists on the dignity of the Virgin Mary and holds that her virginity was "preserved in a miraculous way." Francisco Suárez, S.J. (1548-1617) treated the question extensively. He reports the variety of objections and conclusions that had been put forward, ascribing to Erasmus of Rotterdam the heresy that - for physical reasons - the mother could not have remained a virgin while giving birth. Suárez's conclusion is that through God's will in the act of giving birth to the

child "some parts of its body may have penetrated some other parts of the virgin's body, however in a way that this did not include imperfection nor deny the truth of the birth ... so that Christ exited the uterus of his mother in an ineffable and ununderstandable way, so that it befits Christian modesty not to inquire further into details" (Suárez, *Commentariorum*, disp. 5, sect. 2, quotation from p. 78).

17. 50 **Medium...porrigam**, "I will...broad": Stratocles here refers to extending the middle finger, an aggressive and obscene gesture that meant for the Romans the same as it means for us. This phrase is found in Martial's *Epigrams*, Book II, 28: **Rideto multum qui te, Sexille, cinaedum dixerit et digitum porrigito medium**. "Laugh loudly, Sextillus, when someone calls you a queen and put your middle finger out." (Trans. D. R. Shackleton Bailey. Cambridge: Harvard UP, 1993). Cf. Persius, *Satire* 5.119. Closer to Pontanus' time, it is also found in Eramus' *De bello Turcico*, in *Opera* V 3, p. 32, line 29-30: **Domino nos castiganti oppedere, mediumque quod dici solet, digitum ostendere**? "... farting at the Lord, and, as the saying goes, giving him the finger as he seeks to correct us?" (*Collected Works*, vol. 64. trans. Heath). The proverbial character of the gesture is shown by the fact that Erasmus has an entry for it at *Adagia* 1358 = II.4.68 **Medium ostendere digitum**, "to show the middle finger."

18. 51-54 **Rhetor**, "orator": Like a good student of rhetoric, Stratocles here moves on to the next in his list of subjects, i.e., oratory. He refers to the practice of accomplished students who regularly gave speeches in Latin to show off their skills in the language. Both orations and plays would be performed at the opening and closing of the school year, or in celebration of major events within the school or community (McCabe 15).

19. 55-56 **Et Logicus ... condidi**, "I ... logic ... solecisms ... syllogisms": Stratocles is making a pun based on the curriculum of the trivium: grammar, rhetoric and logic. A syllogism is a logical construct developed by Aristotle: it is formed of a "major premise" and a "conclusion," with a second premise (the "minor premise" or "middle term") that joins the two. Example: All mortal things die. All men are mortal things. All men die. A solecism is defined by Aristotle as a logical flaw based on a grammatical error which makes "the opponent appear to be speaking like a barbarian." (Aristotle, *De sophisticis elenchis*, chap. 3, 165 b 21p; in the translation of Giulio Pace, which was available at Pontanus' time: **ut barbare loquatur** [*Aristoteles Latine*, ed. Eckhard Keßler (München: Fink, 1995)]). Stratocles could mean two things here: "Instead of proper arguments I ran into fallacies;" or: "Instead of making arguments I babbled." His pun also implies that he has not progressed beyond the stage where he would be flogged for making such errors. Cf. Lagerlund. For philosophy teaching in Dillingen, including Pontanus, see Leinsle 2006 *Dilinganae* 139-146.

20. 57 **quasi ... introduxerim**, "As if ... things": Literally this reads "as if I were the first to have introduced this way/mode (of doing things)." Stratocles is addressing his fellow students and reminds them that he is giving his own special view of a curriculum already known in its broad outlines by the audience. Those readers or listeners who knew about Pontanus' work in drawing up the official plans for Jesuit education would have found this a nice "inside joke."

21. 59 **quindecim**, "fifteen": See our note above on line 23 **quindecim**.

22. 60-62 Stratocles uses high tragic rhetoric here to describe his time studying philosophy. This could be another way of characterizing him as educationally inept, for he is mixing up his genres or areas of study.

23. 66 **exculpsi ... aquam**, "wrung out ... stone": **Exsculpo** is found first and most often in Plautus, and in other early writers of comedy or satire. It may set up the later joke in line 69 about digging out Aristotle's eyes (**effoderem**), since both verbs convey notions of digging, scratching, or excavating. Cf. Plautus' *Cistellaria* 541 **vix exculpsi, ut diceret**, "With difficulty have I extorted it from her that she should tell me" (Trans. Henry Thomas Riley, p. 197). The last part of the line gives a proverbial expression for impossibility: **ex pumicibus aquam**: cf. Plautus' *Persa* 41 (and also Erasmus, *Adagia* 375 = I.4.75) **nam tu aquam a pumice nunc postulas** "for you are demanding water from a stone."

24. 74 **quis ... nesciunt**, "don't know ... idiocy": This is a parody of a line of questioning that was much loved in the middle ages: who was the inventor of a specific thing (cf. Seneca, *Letters* (= *Ep.*) 88.39)? Stratocles is asking who the "inventor" of stupidity was. Our translation makes reference to this tradition: the literal translation of this line is "who was the first of the fools".

25. 76-77 **Literarum studiis ... inhumanius**, "more inhuman than the humanities": We translate **literarum studiis**, literally "study of literature", as "humanities", in order to bring out a pun with **inhumanius**, "more inhumane". Pontanus the humanist eloquently defended humanistic education in Jesuit schools: see appendix on Humanistic Schools.

26. 89 **vitam perdo ... pecuniam**, "ruining ... destroying ... wasting my money": Here Pontanus uses a rhetorical device called zeugma, which means in Greek "a yoking," as when one hitches two different animals to one plow. In this device one word has more than one object, but the meaning of the word changes with each object, as in, "He arrived in a taxi and a hurry". Here, **perdo** takes **vitam, pecuniam** and **gloriam** all as its objects, each meaning something slightly different; ergo, we use different verbs to convey this play on words. The same device is used below

in A3.48, but there it works in English, so we use only one translation for the use of **evertet** with two objects.

27. 92 **in latrinis faxo iaceas**, "make sure ... latrine": There is a strong contrast between expression and content here. Stratocles uses archaic, quasi-legal diction (**faxo iaceas**) to convey the vulgar notion that he'll "toss in the toilet" any book he sees again.

28. 96-97 **Frequenter ... sollenne ... vesperam**:, "religiously skip school ... evening": The vocabulary is highly ironical. **Sollemnis** is used of a regularly observed religious practice, but Stratocles uses it to describe both his *absence* from school and his drinking in the evening (**ad vesperam**) when he should probably be at *vespers*.

29. 105 **edictabo**, "I'll lecture": We translate **edictabo** here as "lecture" in accordance with Plautus' usage of **edicto** as "speaking openly or publicly," almost "proclaim." Similar uses occur at *Amphitruo* 816; *Epidicus* 105; *Menaechmi* 642. Given the "scholastic" setting and Stratocles' sarcastic response to his teacher, "lecture" seems a good fit here.

30. 113-114 **fabulor ... fabulam**, "telling you ... telling tall tales": There is some wordplay here with **fabulor**, a verb meaning both "converse" and "invent a story", and **fabula**, a noun which can mean gossip, legend, a fable or (*OLD* **fabula** 6) a play or a piece of theater. Eubulus engages in some meta-theatrical repartee. Cf. 116 **fabulatur fabulas**, "telling tall tales".

31. 121 **Canibus et volucribus ... convivium**, "feast for dogs and vultures": Reference to Homer, *Iliad* 1.5-6, where the same metaphor occurs.

32. 122 **sine fuco**, "without pretence or fakery" is a proverbial phrase for "speaking plainly" (*OLD* **fucus** 4).

33. 126 **Orcus**, "Hades": Orcus is a standard term for the underworld, which we choose to render as the more familiar "Hades". Stratocles' riposte of "sending many down to Hades" is a reference to Homer, *Iliad* 1.3. Stratocles thus makes a properly literary reply to Eubulus' earlier allusion to the *Iliad* (see note on 121). Any reader of ancient literature would have recognized **hac ... dextra** "this right hand" as referring to the sword arm.

34. 129 **inviti ... nolumus**, "unwilling ... happen": A reformulation in the negative of a phrase that had become proverbial, taken from Caesar, *Civil War* 2.27 **nam, quae volumus, et credimus libenter**, "for what we want, we also willingly believe".

35. 135-6 **me ... concinnare postulas**, "you're trying ... words": The Latin is odd here, probably owing to Pontanus' attempt to work in a quotation from Plautus' *Captivi* 601 **me insanum verbis concinnat suis** "she's driving me insane with her words". This use of **concinno** with a predicate adjective meaning "to make or render x" seems to be a particularly Plautine usage. Pontanus completed his own edition of the *Captivi* and knew it well. The use of **postulo** here is also reminiscent of Plautus (*OLD* **postulo** 6).

36. 138 **stulte ... sapienter**, "foolishly ... wisely": Cf. Stratocles' discussion of the fool (**stultus**) vs. the wise man (**sapiens**) in 70-74 above.

37. 139 **reduco calculum**, "correct my error": **Reducere calculum** is an arithmetical metaphor. **Ponere calculum**, to "place a stone", as on an abacus or counting board, means "make an argument"; **reducere** (pull back, change) **calculum** hence means "change a line of reasoning that is unsatisfactory".

38. 152-155 **proverbio ... dare**, "proverb ... enlist in the military": There are many handbooks of sayings in German and Latin (some included in the bibliography) that include these three commitments as things to be avoided or only entered into after careful consideration (the other common one is a sea voyage). See, e.g., Binder #2294. Pontanus himself contributed to the "genre" of tracts against marriage with his own *De conubii miseriis*, "The miseries of marriage".

39. 159 **eventus ... magister est**, "experience is the teacher of fools": This is a clear reference to Livy 22.39 **Nec eventus modo hoc docet – stultorum iste magister est**, "not only does experience teach this – that indeed is the teacher of fools ...". The allusion is appropriately chosen, since in this passage in Livy the famous general Quintus Fabius Maximus Cunctator (the "delayer" and eventual victor over Hannibal; see below our note on A4.77) counsels *against* combat.

40. 163-167: Cf. Erasmus, *Soldier and Carthusian* p. 192 Thompson (*Collected Works* vol. 39), where many of the same points are enumerated.

41. 176 **numismata cudentur**, "coins ... struck": Ancient coins were not cast with molten metal but "struck". Slugs of soft metal (gold, silver, bronze) were placed between two intaglio (i.e., with the images carved in reverse) molds, and a hammer blow would imprint the designs for both sides of the coin on the metal. Pontanus is making an association between generals' "minting" money by exploiting soldiers' labor and the corporal punishment (like the blows of struck coins) suffered by soldiers.

42. 182-188 **tonsoribus ... chirurgos**, "barbers ... surgeons like that": In the sixteenth century the majority of "surgeons" were in fact barbers; many invasive procedures were done by those with training closer to that of craftsmen than of academically trained physicians. For example, blood-letting as medical therapy (like that mentioned in lines 185-187) figured prominently in medicine from antiquity to the eighteenth century, and was not always practiced skillfully, especially on the battlefield. Strato-cles' use of the respectable term "surgeons" after Eubulus' description of battlefield medicine practiced by "barbers" shows that he is woefully ignorant of what awaits him on campaign.

43. 189 ff.: Eubulus' speech contains many standard topics about the sol-dier's life. Pontanus discusses these also in *Institutiones* 3.222-223, where in a discussion of honorific poems he lists the things one conventionally praises about soldiers: obedience towards leaders, sentry duty at night, enduring heat, cold, marches, hunger, thirst, the control of appetites, and the love of country and victory, especially as proven through the exhibi-tion of wounds and scars.

44. 190-191 **arma horrida ... gravissima**, "bristling arms ... bear": The ad-jective **horridus** has meanings ranging from "bristling", i.e., with the hairs on one's neck standing up, to "horrid", i.e., "something that *makes* the hair on the neck stand up." Arms can "bristle" in the sense of rows of spears standing up like the bristles on a boar's back, and also inspire "hair-raising" fear. This and the following line are probably veiled allu-sions to *Aeneid* 6.86-7, **bella, horrida bella .... cerno**, "I forsee wars, ter-rible wars". Pontanus repeats **arma** as Vergil repeats **bella**, and the **aenea** "bronze" in line 191 may pun on the hero's name, Aeneas, but also refer to his famous bronze shield as depicted in *Aeneid* 8. The description of the weapons as "hard to bear" is our attempt to render a pun in Latin that is similar to one in English: **gravis** (see **gravissima** 191) can mean both "physically heavy" as well as "weighty, grave, serious."

45. 199 **communis ... exitus**, "Mars ... uncertain": These are famous com-monplaces about the unpredictability of war that were taken from Clas-sical literature and made proverbial in the centuries prior to Pontanus. Cf. Cicero's *Pro Marcello* (*Marc.*) 5.14 **incertus exitus et anceps fortuna belli**, "uncertain is the outcome and ambiguous the fortune of war"; *Let-ters to his Friends* (*Fam.*) 6.4.1 **cum omnis belli Mars communis et cum semper incerti exitus proeliorum sunt**, "since Mars is the same in every war and the outcomes of battles are always uncertain." Cf. **Mars commu-nis** in Erasmus, *Adagia* 3649 = IV.7.49. Erasmus notes that this proverb was picked out of Homer (*Iliad*, 6.339, 18.309) by Aristotle in his *Rheto-ric* (2.2.11). This sentiment was also echoed multiple times by Livy (*From the Founding of the City*, 2.40.14, 7.29.2, 8.23.8, 8.31.5, 9.44.8, 25.19.5, 30.30.20), and Cicero includes the idea in his *Philippics* (10.10.20).

46. 205-206 **Solon**, "Solon": This is a kind of scholarly footnote delivered in mid-speech by the ostentatiously pedantic Eubulus. The observation was famous: cf. Cicero, *On Old Age* = *Cato maior* 20.73: **Solonis quidem sapientis elogium est, quo se negat velle suam mortem dolore amicorum et lamentis vacare** "This indeed is the saying of Solon the wise, in which he says he does not want his own death to be empty of the grief and laments of friends."

47. 207 **Esto ... patriam**, "Should ... fatherland": The syntax here is odd, perhaps to reflect Eubulus' pedantry (see note on 205-6) and also to underscore the highly unlikely prospect of someone returning unwounded. Literally, "Let it, however, happen that someone be returned into the fatherland."

48. 210-212 **Plenus dorsus ... inhonesto vulnere**, "back ... wounds": In the Latin these mutilations are said to comprise a single wound, but we have rendered it as a plural to avoid confusion.

49. 213-215 **Interea coniunx ... misericordia**, "Meanwhile ... pity": See Faustina's version of these themes in her speech A.3.40-57.

50. 218 **Bellum ... inexpertis**, "War ... inexperienced:" Cf. Erasmus, *Adagia* 951 = IV.1.1: *Dulce bellum inexpertis*. Erasmus concisely phrases this proverb but notes that the sentiment had also been formulated by Vegetius (*De re militari*, 3.12), Pindar (fragment), and Horace (*Epistles*, 1.18.86-87). Pontanus here (with slight variation) quotes the title of Erasmus' essay on war, to which he alludes often and which served as a source for much of the material for this play. We chose to acknowledge the importance of Erasmus' essay by citing it in Latin and treating it as a famous title that we then translate.

51. 220-224 **nullum .. bellum geri ... debet**, "war never be waged ... necessary": See the section of the introduction on just war for more information on these arguments and their history.

52. 224 **praestanti mactos indole**, "blessed ... excellence": **Macte** is an old form sometimes used in direct address to deities, but most often to distinguished males, meaning "be blessed or honored for x," where x is usually some physical or mental quality of benefit on the battlefield. Cf. Silius Italicus, *Punica* 4.475 (to a young, distinguished military leader): **macte, o macte indole sacra**, "(boy), honor (to you), be honored for your sacred nature/talent"; Erasmus, *Letters* (= *Epist.*) 58 (1497), to one of his students: **macte ... adolescens ... praestanti ... indoli**, "honored young man with outstanding natural qualities".

53. 231-2 **Tua dicta ... desistere**, "your words ... started": We have changed

the punctuation from Rädle's edition, which places a period at the end of 231 and a comma after **trado**. He translates as we do but does not alter the punctuation in the Latin. The last three words of 232 are probably a double allusion, the first to Vergil, *Aen.* 1.37 **mene incepto desistere**, "am I to step away from what I've started?" The second reference is more likely, to the *Dicta* (later *Disticha*) *Catonis*, "The Sayings of Cato". This collection of Latin verse sayings and apothegms was first produced probably in the fourth century CE and later became very popular as a school text that was used both to teach Latin style and to instill moral precepts in European schoolboys. Pontanus would have known them well; Erasmus and Scaliger, two famous scholars, both produced editions of the collection. Cf. *Disticha* 1.9 **Cumque moneas aliquem nec se velit ille moneri, / si tibi sit carus, noli desistere coeptis**, "When you give someone a warning and he doesn't want to be advised, if you like him, don't stop what you've begun."

54. 234 **Sive potius ... Deus**, "or rather ... God": We depart from Rädle's text here, which prints **cupido sit Deus**, "let my desire be God". This must be a typographical error in Rädle's edition, since there is no indication of any variants in his apparatus criticus. However, in the earliest witness to the text from 1578 (M2: see introduction on history of the text) **fit** is clearly read, as it is in A, the 1594 version printed in Ingolstadt (p. 573 line 24). The indicative **fit**, "becomes", is superior on two counts. First, it maintains a parallel construction with the **sive ... iniecta est** of the previous line, and an otherwise unmotivated switch to a subjunctive is difficult to construe. Second, this line is a clear allusion to an apposite passage in Vergil, *Aeneid* 9.184-185. In that section Nisus and Euryalus, two young warriors eager for combat, discuss their burning ambition to embark on what they hope will be a glorious expedition. In the sequel they are both tragically killed. Before they leave, **Nisus ait: 'dine hunc ardorem mentibus addunt, / Euryale, an sua cuique deus fit dira cupido?** "Nisus says, 'Are the gods putting this passion in my mind, Euryalus, or does his own dreadful desire become each man's god?'" In his adaptation, Pontanus has changed "are the gods putting" to "divinely inspired" (**divinitus**) and changed the alternative question from **ne ... an** to **sive ... sive**. The close correspondence between the ends of lines 185 in Vergil and 234 in Pontanus argue strongly for an intentional allusion and thus for a change in the text (which also increases the coherence of the line). What could be read as a theologically problematic line is thus best understood as an allusion to Vergil that has deep thematic resonance: Stratocles is echoing the thoughts of a famously eager warrior whose ambition for glory led to his own death and the death of his closest friend.

55. 235 **taratantaram**, "blare of the trumpet": Pontanus quotes a very rare

and famous onomatopoetic neologism coined to reproduce the sound of a war trumpet at Ennius, *Annales* 140.

56. 237 **Nobile facinus**, "noble deed": Stratocles' lofty rhetoric here may include an allusion to Cicero, *Against Verres* (= *Ver.*) 2.82, where this phrase is used sarcastically to introduce a description of one of Verres' most notorious crimes.

57. 238 **in pluma ... emori**, "to die .. petals": This is roughly equivalent to the English phrase "in the lap of luxury". **Pluma**, "feather", used in metonomy for pillows, and rose petals (**rosa**), were shorthand for the luxuries available only to the decadent rich, and are often contrasted with military hardships. Cf. Sen. *Dialogues* (= *Dial.*) 1.3.10; Cicero, *Tusculan Disputations* 5.73.

58. 241-243: These lines are likely a reference to the stern moral code of the Stoics. Neo-Stoicism enjoyed a significant flowering in these years, fostered by Pontanus' contemporary Justus Lipsius, a great scholar, humanist, philosopher and advisor to rulers (and also a strong nationalist; cf. line 244).

59. 248 **fortissimum ducem**, "a man of decisive action": Literally, "the bravest leader". We opt for this translation to make clear the contrast between brave action in the field and decadent inaction at home. The phrase **fortissimum ducem** is used of a Greek general in Pontanus' remarks on how to compose honorific poems for military leaders in *Institutiones* 3.223; see above, note 189 ff.

60. 254 **virtutis ... instrumenta**, "makings of manliness": **Instrumentum** in Latin often means the equipment or means for a specific task or purpose (*OLD* **instrumentum** 1; 3). Stratocles here quotes Cicero again: Cicero, *Against Catiline* (= *Catil.*) 2.9 **adsuefactus frigore et fame et siti et vigiliis perferendis fortis ab istis praedicabatur, cum industriae subsidia atque instrumenta virtutis in libidine audaciaque consumeret,** "... since he was used to enduring cold and hunger and thirst and night watches he was extolled by them as brave, although he was squandering through lust and reckless conduct the aids to action and the makings of manliness." This passage describes Catiline as personally gifted but corrupt and selfish. Stratocles quotes Cicero "out of context" to construct his justifications for going to war: those familiar with the original context know that these words describe one of Rome's most notorious traitors.

61. 256 **morbi**, "diseases": cf. Eubulus' remarks in 196-197 above. Stratocles, like a good student of rhetoric, is responding point by point to the arguments offered by his teacher.

62. 257 **pestilitas**, "plague": Pontanus' knowledge of Latin is again on display here: Stratocles uses a rare poetic word instead of the much more
normal **pestilentia**, which comes directly into English. The word occurs
first in Classical Latin in a discussion on the nature of diseases in Lucretius' long poem on Nature, *De Rerum Natura* 6.1098; 1125; 1132.

63. 258 **vos**, "none of you here": Stratocles moves to the plural, "you all";
this may indicate an aside or an attempt by Pontanus to generalize these
comments to the student audience.

64. 276 **redde natum**, "return my son": This is probably an allusion to Ovid,
Fasti 2.485 **redde patri natum**, "return the son to his father". It is not
clear why more children are mentioned in the next phrase (**liberos**, "children (sons)").

65. 290 **collimet scopum**, "hit the target": The metaphor is from archery.
This is a post-classical phrase based probably on the latinization of the
Greek word for target, **scopos** (see *OLD* **scopulus**), and a change in pro-
nunciation and spelling of the Classical **collinio**, "to aim". The phrase
occurs in a dialogue on the administration of the area of Transylvania
penned in 1584 by the humanist Farkas Kovacsóczy. Pontanus may have
known his work, or vice versa, for in that dialogue the "teacher" is also
called Eubulus. See the section of the introduction on characters' names,
and bibliography under Kovacsóczy for more information.

66. 292 **viribus**, "their own strength": **Vis** (also commonly **vires** in the plural) has a wide range of meanings in Latin. Here it is closest to "physical
powers" or "vigor" (*OLD* **vis** 20-21, but see also 14, 15, 17, 22).

67. 297 **corvum ... candidum**, "white raven": An impossible animal that was
proverbial for "something impossible", like the contemporary American
phrases "when hell freezes over" or "when pigs fly". Cf. Erasmus, *Adagia*
3635 = IV.7.35.

68. 298 **errabit parum**, "only a little off the mark": The Latin verb **erro**
is often used for "mistake, be wrong"; we opted for "miss the mark" to
continue the archery motif introduced in 290.

69. 305 **In vitium ... facillime**, "like wax ... is bent ... toward vice": With
this adaptation of a line from Horace Eubulus starts his disquisition on
the shortcomings of youth that is heavily indebted in both ideas and
phrasing to Horace's *Art of Poetry* 156-165. In that section Horace gives
instructions on how to draw youthful characters in drama, and Pontanus
relies heavily on these remarks of Horace when he writes on theater in
his *Institutiones*. Cf. Horace, *Art of Poetry* (= *Ars*) 163 **cereus in vitium
flecti**, "[a young man] like wax is bent toward vice"; cf. also appendix on
writing drama.

70. 307 **somniat**, "dreams": **Somnio** is used of normal dreaming as well as "day dreaming" and "having delusions".

71. 311 **Canibus ... maxime**, "greatest joy ... horses": These were emblematic aristocratic pursuits. This line is also taken from Horace's *Art of Poetry* 162 **gaudet equis canibusque**, "rejoices in horses and dogs"; cf. the note above on 305.

72. 314-315 **Spernit Junonem ... iudicat**, "Scorns Juno ... judges": This is an allusion to the cause of the Trojan war, the "judgement of Paris", a Trojan prince who chose the goddess of Love, Venus, as the most beautiful goddess and spurned Juno and Athena. Cf., e.g., Ovid, *Heroides* (also sometimes called *Letters* = *Ep.*) 16,133 ff. Paris was a notoriously un-warlike voluptuary. Juno here is best understood as the goddess of heavenly rule and Athena as goddess of wisdom.

73. 318 **Molles ... iocos**, "Gentle laughter ... flirtatious jokes": **Molles** is repeated in this line, and we render it by both "gentle" and "flirtatious". Both of those notions were associated with effeminacy or women in Classical literature and are here intended as contrasts to serious martial virtues.

74. 323 **tantum ... habet**, "unrestrained": This is our rendering for what is literally "he offers as much as he has".

75. 324 **maioris ... spes**, "hopes ... higher": **maioris** is strictly "larger, greater", but we choose "higher" to match the English idiom with "hopes".

76. 325 **multum**, "overly": **multum** here seems clearly to mean **nimium** ("too much"), so we translate "overly".

77. 331 **Inducere ... fraudem**, "introduce them to deceit": The Latin **induco** allows for both active and passive deception: one can both teach or induce youth to commit deceptions themselves, and one can also fool them. We decided on "introduce them to deceit" to retain that ambiguity.

78. 332 **circumscribuntur**, "fool": Like **induco** in the previous line, **circumscribo** is often found in teaching contexts (*OLD* 2-4, 7). Its use to mean "fool, deceive" (*OLD* 6) is less common.

79. 335-338 **Iamque ... potest**, "First ... can say": Our rendering, with its many commas, reflects the somewhat awkward syntax of the original. It is as if Eubulus is adding many reformulations or afterthoughts as he goes along.

80. 337-338 **Explodit ... bombardulam**, "fires ... weapon": This stage direction appears in Latin in the original. Cf. Stratocles' exit and his remarks at line 287.

81. 338-341 **Magister, syllogismus...dabit**, "Teacher, this was the right syllogism...solve everything": Again, Stratocles mocks syllogisms, specifically Eubulus' attempts to use logic to persuade his student against war. In lines 338-341, Stratocles refers to the **propositio maior** (the major premise), **propositio minor** (minor premise/middle term), and **conclusio** (conclusion). See note at lines 55-56 for more information.

82. 345-346 **dissectae ... dissectus**, "tattered .... skewered": The Latin uses the same verb for all three articles of clothing mentioned, but that much repetition is unpleasant in English, so we render different nuances of the verb for each noun. We repeat each verb below in 347 in order to heighten the rhetorical effect, although the Latin has only the one form.

83. 352 **fugitor**, "deserter": Pontanus is showing off his knowledge of Latin. The word **fugitor**, "deserter," appears in extant Latin in antiquity only once, in Plautus' *Trinummus* 723. The character Stasimus criticizes his master Lesbonicus, **Credo ad summos bellatores acrem fugitorem fore**, "I believe that he will be a fierce deserter among the greatest warriors." Cf. our notes on 437 **Praeclari bellatores** and 475 **bellatores**.

84. 355 **opimis ... spoliis**, "splendid spoils": This is a ridiculously grandiloquent claim for anyone who actually knew Roman history. The **spolia opima** were properly the arms of an enemy king that were stripped by the victorious Roman leader after victory in single combat. The Romans claimed that this had happened only three times in their history (cf. Livy 4.20 for a fuller account). Stratocles is imagining scenes well beyond his station or capabilities.

85. 369 **avibus quam faelicissimis**, "the most favorable of omens": literally, "under the most fortunate birds possible". See *OLD* **avis** 3, "a bird as an omen or source of omens". Augurs (a special kind of priest) would examine the flight direction and/or eating patterns of birds to discern the gods' will, i.e., whether the undertaking in question was blessed by the gods or did not meet with their approval. This was normal practice for the Romans.

86. 369-370: The answers Stratocles gives here change in the various versions, depending on the historical situation at the time. See the section of the introduction on the wars of the sixteenth century for a full explanation. Compare similar variants at verse 552.

87. 371 **Thrasonice**, "Thraso": Literally, "like Thraso, Thrasonically". Thraso was a famous comic character. We contemplated attempting to update the metaphor with something more contemporary like "Rambo" or more readily recognizeable like "Achilles", but settled for an older reference. In the comic playwright Terence's *Eunuchus*, Thraso is a soldier and a lover of the prostitute Thais. He greatly exaggerates his social, physical, and mental prowess, and is an example of the stock character of the braggart soldier. Yet, when he and his cohorts storm Thais' house, he places himself in the rear of the attacking force, claiming that this arrangement of forces is effective tactics and good generalship. His sarcastic hanger-on Gnatho remarks in an aside, however, that this "strategy" is simply a symptom of Thraso's true cowardice (line 783). Pontanus has Eubulus call Stratocles "Thraso" here in order to imply that Stratocles' boasts are as empty and exaggerated as Thraso's, and that in fact he, like Thraso, will prove to be a coward when faced with violence. For fuller remarks see the edition by John Barsby.

88. 375-381: Here Stratocles uses language that both confesses a sin to Eubulus and begs his forgiveness for that sin. However, although this seems to allude to the Catholic Sacrament of Reconciliation (i.e., confession), it is more likely that Stratocles is making an appeal to the humanistic nature of Eubulus, by asking him to forgive him humanely (**condones humaniter**). However, a similar scene between a husband and wife later in the play clearly refers to the Catholic Sacrament, beginning in line A4.78. See our note there for more information.

89. 382-384 **lacrymas ... gratias**: A reference again to Plautus' *Captivi* 419, another expression of heartfelt thanks between friends: **Hominum ingenium liberale! Ut lacrumas excutiunt mihi!** "Humanity's gentlemanly spirit! How it moves me to tears!"

90. 389 **Deus te servet**, "May God preserve you": In earlier manuscript versions (M2 from 1578 and M5 from 1580: see introduction on history of the text), this phrase was **Dii servent**, and **Dii te servassint**, both meaning "may the gods protect you." However, in our later version, Pontanus changes this to **Deus te servet**, "may God protect you." This also occurs at line 208: in the earlier manuscripts, the phrase was **dii immortales**, "immortal gods," but in our later version it reads **Deum Immortalem**, "Immortal God." Cf. A4.89 below. In both of these instances, Pontanus makes a change from a lower-case, plural g-, in favor of a capitalized, singular G-. It seems that in this later version Pontanus makes his characters refer to the Christian God more often. It is interesting that both of these revisions are lines spoken by Eubulus, the most educated character in the play.

91. See introduction on history of the text for more specifics on these insertions for the performance on Mardi Gras. M5 is our only witness for the material in what Rädle included as appendices. Like most handwritten documents from this period it has various abbreviations that Rädle expands. The spelling is not uniform, and there are many common deviations from what we have come to view as orthography. We did not think it important to mark or comment upon these deviations in spelling (e.g., A.1.4 **hyberno** for the more standard **hiberno**).

92. A1.12 **Potestas fit**, "you have the right": **Potestas** is strictly the power or authority possessed by a general or magistrate (*OLD* **potestas** 1; 3), and can also mean the opportunity or right to enjoy or use something, as here (*OLD* **potestas** 5). Stratocles seems to imagine himself as a general; as with the **spolia opima** in 355 above he uses vocabulary that is above his station and envisions privileges that are highly improbable.

93. A1.18 **Et ... largius**, "generously ... dinner": There is a joke about manners here, and a pun. Generosity was thought to be a "liberal" quality associated with noble and well-bred men. Such men do not invite themselves to dinner. Stratocles says that his fellow students do just that, but "generously/lavishly", i.e. in an unrestrained way, not in a "gentlemanly" way.

94. A1.19 **glires**, "dormice": **Glires** or dormice were a kind of small rodent raised and fattened in captivity by the Romans and served as a delicacy.

95. A1.20 **E stativis ... egredi**, "to leave our quarters": Stratocles is describing student life with military vocabulary: one of the chief meanings of **egredior** is "to march out" as if to battle (*OLD* 1b), and **stativus** in the plural often means a camp or garrison (*OLD* **stativus** 2).

96. A1.21-22 **Gallinis ... vulpes ... iucundissime**, "fox ... hounds": Hunting vocabulary is commonly used of sexual or amorous pursuit in Latin literature. Pontanus could have counted on lots of laughs from these lines.

97. A1.23 **nasus est mere sagax / odorator**, "nose ... keen-scented purebred bloodhound": **Odorator** is a post-classical word for bloodhound. The primary meaning of **sagax** is "keen-scented" (*OLD* 1). We accept with Rädle the reading **mere**, "purely", which we translate as "purebred", in preference to the reading in M5, **mire**, "amazingly", which does not fit the context well.

98. A1.24 **videt**, "picks up": **Videt** means "sees". We translate "picks up" in order to maintain the hunting metaphor. Humans, however, "hunt" erotically with the eyes, not the nose. The stark contrast in metaphor (smell

switching quickly to sight) reveals the non-literal nature of Stratocles'
remarks about "hunting".

99. 397 **Herculis**, "Hercules": Hercules was the strongest of ancient fight-
ers. Stratocles seems to be modelling his fighting stance after statuary,
not military trainers. He thus exposes the shallow, "bookish" nature of
his visions of military life.

100. 402 **Multorum ... rimabitur**, "blade ... many": Pontanus parades his
learning here. This line appears to be a combination of a line from a very
obscure poem on the Trojan war, Baebius Italicus' (1ˢᵗ cent. CE) *Ilias* 456
rimabant inimico corpora ferro "they gashed the bodies with hostile
swords" and Vergil, *Aeneid* 6.599 **viscera rimatur**, "roots around in his
vitals" (of the bird pecking at Prometheus' liver). The primary meaning of **rimor** is to examine carefully with the eyes, especially fissures or
crevasses; only rarely and in poets does it mean "cut" or "put furrows in"
(see *OLD* **rimor**). Once again Stratocles reveals his merely "armchair"
knowledge of combat. Given the double allusion, we translate "will root
about in"; it is graphically disturbing when used of a sword, and conveys
some part of the primary meaning of "to scrutinize, probe".

101. 403 **Unde ... sanguine**, "where the brains ... blood": Stratocles seems
to imagine himself stabbing people by turns in the guts and the head.
In contrast to Stratocles' muddled understanding of battle is Pontanus'
deep knowledge of literature. This line, like the one above it, is probably an adaptation of material from fairly obscure writers. Cf. Velleius
Paterculus 2.120.6, a story of an aristocratic Roman soldier captured by
Germans who committed suicide by bashing his shackles against his
own head so hard that he fractured his skull and **protinus pariter san-
guinis cerebrique profluvio expiraret**, "immediately he expired from
the outflow of blood and brain".

102. 407 **Cadentum ... sidera**, "groans ... stars": This is a clear allusion to
Vergil *Aen.* 10.674 **gemitum cadentum**, "the moaning of those falling"
and 11.37 **ingentem gemitum tunsis ad sidera tollent / Pectoribus ...**
"from their beaten breasts they will raise to the stars a huge groan".

103. 412 **pedibus ... timor**, "fear ... feet": Another reference to Vergil:
Aen. 8.224 **pedibus timor addidit alas** "fear added wings to their feet".
When confronted with genuine fear, Stratocles retreats to what he really
knows, namely poetry: i.e., he knows school, not war.

104. A.3.10-11 **adipisci ... adepti sunt**, "obtain ... attain": We translate in
this way in order to render Pontanus' use of two different forms of the
verb **adipiscor**, "get, obtain". Debate on the merits of marriage was a
common rhetorical exercise: Pontanus wrote a dialogue *De conubii mis-*

eriis ("The Woes of Marriage"), which exists in a 1990 edition by Rädle.

105. A3.17 **una ... penatibus**, "under the same roof": The Latin refers to **penates**, tutelary deities of the house and property (somewhat similar in appearance and demeanor to leprechauns) that were regularly used as a metaphor in Latin literature for "household, hearth and home". Note the correspondence between the six years of Faustina's travails and the six-year period of toil mentioned by Stratocles in his opening lament on student life.

106. A3.18 **quia meminisse ... animus**, "because my spirit quails at the memory": Faustina quotes Vergil here, referencing Aeneas' response to Dido's request that he tell of the sack of Troy. Pontanus puts in the mouth of the abandoned woman the words in Vergil's poem that are spoken *by* the suffering hero *to* the soon-to-be-abandoned woman: *Aen.* 2,12 **quamquam animus meminisse horret luctuque refugit**, "although my spirit shudders at the memory and recoils in grief."

107. A3.28-29 **nescio ... Exagitatus**, "driven on ... torment": Cf. Plautus, *Aulularia* 631 **quae te mala crux agitat?** "which bad cross is bothering/harassing you ..."; same at *Bacchides* 584. **Mala crux** is used often in Plautus to mean "torment".

108. A3.31 **qui temperas...machinam**, "you who control...with a single nod": This refers to Jupiter, who is referenced by many Classical authors as having the ability to govern the fates of men with a simple nod. In Homer's *Iliad*, Zeus (Jupiter) says that bowing his head is the "strongest sign among the immortal gods" and so "nothing can be revoked or left unfinished." The very act itself shakes the foundations of Mt. Olympus (Hom. *Il.* 1.515-530). For other descriptions that convey this image cf. Vergil *Aeneid* 10.112-116; Catullus 64.204-206; *Homeric Hymns* "To Dionysus," 13-16.

109. A3.39, **dotem**, "dowry:" According to Roman custom, a husband became the steward of his wife's dowry. Upon his death or in the case of divorce, however, the dowry would be returned to the wife as her own property. Only an irresponsible husband would spend his wife's dowry, because, if he were to die, his own property could be sold to repay the dowry he had spent (Treggiari 327-329). Likewise, in order to prevent strain in a marriage or legal troubles in the case of divorce, Augustus' adultery law placed restrictions on the husband's right to dispose of his wife's dowry (Grubb 96). Here Misomachus is portrayed as a spendthrift and a negligent husband for having spent his wife's dowry. Because he has, Faustina is now forced to sell off the family's property in order to maintain herself and her children. Legal and social norms had obviously changed by Pontanus' time, but it is noteworthy that even by the

standards of ancient Roman law Misomachus' conduct as described here is worthy of strong censure.

110. A3.48 **Aedibus evertere ... omnibus,** "will turn ... fortune": **Evertere** here takes two objects, **aedibus** and **fortunis.** The rhetorical device is called zeugma; see our note above on 89 **perdo,** where we use a different verb for each of the various objects of **perdo;** also below on 551 **sinite.**

111. A.3.52 **qui thorum ambiant meum,** "who are after my marriage bed": **Ambio** can have several meanings: *OLD* 2. to visit (in search of sympathy); 3. to strive for, seek to obtain; 6. to surround, throng. We translate as 'they are after' mostly to convey the third definition (striving for), but also to suggest a crowd or throng.

112. A3.52-53 **Et...desunt,** "And...bed": Faustina's remarks call to mind the plight of Penelope in Homer's *Odyssey.* Penelope, unlike Faustina, desires to keep her many suitors at bay over the many years she awaits the return of her beloved Odysseus. Cf. Hom. *Od.* 19.157-160, where the faithful wife proclaims, "...I cannot escape a marriage, nor can I contrive / a deft way out. My parents urge me to tie the knot / and my son is galled as they squander his estate" (Trans. Robert Fagles, p. 395).

113. A3.56 **nempe,** "presumably": We translate **nempe** here as "presumably" in the "if-clause" of a future less vivid condition (cf. *OLD,* **nempe** 1c).

114. A3.59 **Leaenam aut Tygridem,** "Lioness or Tigress": Faustina is comparing herself with a lioness and tigress to convey the ferocity and the savagery with which she attacks her husband Misomachus. Ancient authors often compared scorned and furious women with lionesses and other wild or mythological beasts. Catullus (60.1-2) compares a woman to a lioness of the Libyan mountains and a "barking Scylla." Moreover, Pontanus seems to make reference to a common ancient double-entendre. Lioness and Tigress were common pet names given to both low- and high-class prostitutes by their male lovers (Licht 409-410). Thus these lines refer back to Eubulus's remarks that in wartime women sometimes engage in prostitution in order to support themselves and their children (213-215), and anticipate Misomachus' worries about the same.

Faustina's situation would not have been uncommon. In his commentary on the Turkish War, Erasmus (*Consultatio de Bello Turcis Inferendo et Obiter Enarratus Psalmus* 28, p. 213, ed. Baker-Smith *Collected Works* vol. 64) implies that prostitution is a consequence of war: "Nor have we escaped the curse mentioned in Deuteronomy: 'They marry wives and another sleeps with them.' It is now nothing new for us to 'to sow where another shall reap, to plant a vine from which we shall not drink, to have foreigners rule over us.'"

115. A3.62 **seminavit**, "sired": **Semino** means "to sow seed", either agriculturally or sexually. It might also have raised a laugh or two in the audience of this **seminarium** (i.e., *seminary*). Cf. the use of **colo** to mean "cultivate, maintain" marital fidelity in A.4.95-96; there, as here, we have a likely double entendre with another meaning of this verb, "plow" = "have sexual intercourse".

116. 419 **Lares paterni**, "ancestral gods": Misomachus refers to minor divinities that the Romans worshipped in their homes and conceived of as a sort of "guardian spirit" of the land, house and property of individual households; cf. our note above at A3.17 **una ... penatibus** about **penates**, who were similar spirits usually worshipped together with **lares**.

117. 428 **philosophastri**, "foolosophers": This is our (borrowed) rendering of **philosophaster**, a derogatory term meaning something like "pretend or so-called or self-styled philosopher." Pontanus may have taken it from a disparaging remark about Cicero in Augustine, *Civitate Dei*, 2.27, **philosophaster Tullius**, "the so-called philosopher Tullius (= Cicero)." Given his frequent borrowing in this play from Erasmus, it is more likely that Pontanus found the word in the later author: cf. *Antibarbari* 91.677 (= *Opera Omnia*, ord. 1, tom.1, p. 91). We have borrowed the translation "foolosophers" from H.H. Hudson, trans. 1941, p. 10.

118. 432-433 **a morte ... tribus ... distant,** "three fingers from death": This metaphor appears to be proverbial for "very close": cf. Juvenal 12.57-59 **i nunc et ventis animam committe dolato / confisus ligno, digitis a morte remotus / quattuor aut septem** "go, now, and entrust your soul to the winds, relying on a dug out piece of wood (i.e., a ship), removed from death by four or seven fingers ..."

119. 433 **Mars mors o vale, vale,** "Farewell, Mars! Farewell, death!": There is an untranslatable pun here: **Mars mors** is a way of saying that "war (represented by Mars, the patron deity of war) equals death (which is **mors** in Latin)". Wordplay deriving from the changing of a single letter was much beloved by Romans, as evidenced in rhetorical handbooks.

120. 437 **Praeclari bellatores fuimus,** " Magnificent warriors is what we were": We translate **fuimus** as a neutral "were," but the passage has an important precedent. The verb is best understood as fully "perfect" in the sense of "we *were* great soldiers *then* but that is done and we are no longer"; cf. the classic reference **fuimus Troes** "we were/have been (but are no longer) Trojans" at Verg. *Aen.* 2.325. In his note on the line from Vergil in his multi-volume commentary on the *Aeneid* (vol. II, 891-892), Pontanus has a long note on exactly this sense of the word (and its predecessors in Euripides' plays on the fall of Troy). Erasmus also includes

this line it in his *Adagia* 850 = I.9.50, proof of the line's importance and prominence in Pontanus' time. Pontanus surely is consciously using and altering the line here.

121. 438-440 **pediculi**, "lice": These veteran soldiers were schooled well, for here they allude to a famous anecdote and riddle concerning Homer (repeated in many versions in antiquity), one that pokes fun at the lack of intelligence and understanding in artists. Homer fails to understand what two boys who are talking about killing lice mean when they say, "what we saw and caught we left behind, what we didn't see and catch we bring" (Lefkowitz 17-18).

122. 445 **strategemata**, "exploits": Misomachus here uses a Greek word that means "a piece of generalship", but also means "a trick or ruse", a meaning found in Cicero's letters (*Att.* 5.2.2), a body of work much loved and studied by Pontanus.

123. 449 **a notis conscindimur sibilis**, "everyone ... tears ... hisses at us": Literally, "we are torn apart by hisses". The metaphor in Latin is bold: they are torn apart *through* the hissing of people known to them. Cf. Cicero, *Att.* 2.19.3, a letter complaining about how the populace is making fun of the famous general Pompey: **nam gladiatoribus qua dominus qua advocati sibilis conscissi** "as with gladiators, also the master and his advocates are torn apart with hisses".

124. 450 **affatim**, "really": **Affatim** here means something like "to explain it fully, sufficiently" (see *OLD* **affatim**); we opted for the more colloquial "really," which one might say in offering a correction to an earlier definition (as here, where **ludus** has come first).

125. 464 **fabrorum alpha**, "best of all craftsmen": We translate **alpha** (the first letter in the Greek alphabet) as "best"; it is quite literally similar to being on the "A-list". The metaphor has a pedigree. Cf. Martial 2.57.4 (and 5.26.1), in a poem making fun of someone who dresses overly luxuriously: **Cordus alpha paenulatorum** "Cordus, prince/chief/first of those who wear a heavy (foreign) overcoat."

126. 464 **homo horarum omnium**, "a man for all seasons": This is a phrase made famous by Erasmus in a description of Thomas More that appears in a letter of 1521 (letter 1233, p. 297 in Mynors' collection, *Collected Works* vol. 9). It is also found in his *Adages* at 286 (= I.3.86), in Latin essentially identical to that used here by Pontanus.

127. 470 **melius ominare**, "make ... predictions": This is a phrase encountered most often in light classical literature (e.g., comedy or the novel: Plautus, *Rudens* 337; Apuleius, *Met.* 1.22) meaning "to make prognos-

tications". It is close to our phrase "knock on wood". One would use it in response to something unpleasant or threatening that someone else had said, in the hope of "undoing" what was feared to be a predictive utterance.

128. 470-471 **Rem verbis tribus ... effudit**, "one breath ... whole thing": We take some liberties here. The Latin says that he expressed the entire matter "in three words". The verb used, **effundo**, connotes hasty or improvised speech (*OLD* 6). We elected to concentrate on the contrast between the *entire* subject and his expression of it briefly, in *one* breath.

129. 475 **fugitores**, "deserters": See our note on 352 fugitor—a very rare word found in Plautus

130. 481 **indoles**, "natural qualities": This word has connotations of both a person's innate character, disposition or tendency as well as natural excellence (*OLD* **indoles** 1 & 2). We choose "qualities" to convey the second notion in addition to the "inborn" facet we hope is clear in "natural".

131. 487-488 **ex alienis incommodis ... incommoda**, "from another's calamities ... catastrophes": Compare Eubulus' similar remarks in 158-159.

132. 491-492 **In pace ... in bello**, "It is ... peace ... in war": This is a very close adaptation of a line from Sallust, *War with Catiline* 3: **vel pace vel bello clarum fieri licet**, "you can become famous in peace or in war". When Stratocles says "we know this", it is probably his way of saying, "Yes, we've read out Sallust, too (so don't bore us)." Thus Misomachus' rejoinder in 492-493 that his remarks come from personal experience also gains depth: this is not merely bookish advice that he is dispensing.

133. 494-495 **nox ... Abstulerit**, "Night ... day": This appears to be another allusion to Plautus, *Captivi* 415-416: [if I were to remember x], "night would take away the day," **Nox diem adimat**.

134. 498 **ista**, "lousy": The word "lousy" does not appear in the Latin, but **ista** is frequently contemptuous, as here. Given the earlier references to lice, we think it is a good way to render the disparaging tone in this remark.

135. 500 **Ad Persas et Turcas**, "To the Persians and Turks": This is another reference to the contemporary political situation. See the notes at 369 and 552 for more information.

136. 501 **Torquati et annulati et operti purpura**, "torques, rings, and swathed in purple": In 70 B.C. Cicero delivers a series of speeches *In Verrem* (Against Verres) in which he prosecutes Verres, a corrupt gov-

ernor who had plundered the province of Sicily. It was common practice for governors (who acted as generals in their provinces) to reward
their supporters with wealth taken from defeated enemies, but Sicily
had been fully pacified long before, and Verres abused this tradition
in order to benefit himself. Cicero criticizes him for bribing powerful
men in Italy and Sicily with golden rings and torques so they would
not testify against him, thus obscuring his illegal activities (Cic. *Verr.*
3.185-188). Pontanus, who knew Cicero thoroughly, uses this parallel
to portray Stratocles and Polemius as materialistic opportunists rather
than honorable warriors.

Operti purpura refers to purple cloth. Pontanus' language echoes the
words of Isidore of Seville's *Etymologies*: **Trabea erat togae species ex
purpura et cocco qua operti Romanorum reges initio procedebant**,
"The trabea is a type of purple and scarlet toga, draped in which the
first Roman kings used to go out in public" (Isid. *Etym.* 19.24.8). So, by
using this language, Polemius is comparing Stratocles and himself with
royalty, emphasizing their arrogance and desire for riches.

137. 522 **Sexcentos**, "six hundred": See our note above on line 21.

138. 527 **Hanc**, "like this": **Hanc**, "this" here refers unambiguously in the
Latin to the **divina sors** of 526, the bit of divine good fortune that res-
cued him on previous occasions.

139. 535-536 **oculatorum...decem**, "like the speech...ear-witnesses": This
is a clear reference to Plautus, *Truculentus* 489 **pluris est oculatus testis
unus quam auriti decem** "one eye-witness is worth more than ten ear-
witnesses". **Auritus**, "provided with ears, listening, attentive" appears most
often in comic or non-serious authors and contexts (*OLD* **auritus**).

140. 547 **calathos**, "flower baskets": This is a possible reference to Ovid's
Heroides/Letters (= *Ep.)* 9.73. Hercules's wife, Deianira, is reminding him
of all his legendary feats, and here compares him to the time he spent
spinning wool in the women's quarters in Omphale's palace: **Inter Ioni-
acas calathum tenuisse puellas / Diceris,** "you are said to have held a
basket among the Ionian girls." The echo of "calathos", as well as the
contrast between masculine deeds and work reserved for females, make
this a likely and interesting echo.

141. 551 **sinite via**, "get out ... let us": There is a zeugma in this line (see
our note above on 89 **perdo**): **sinite** is used for both "*get out* of our way"
and also "*let* us go".

142. 552-553 **ad Hungaros ... e Belgica**, "for the Hungarians ... from Belgium": Another reference to the contemporary political situation; see
our note above on 369.

143. 554 **Idem Mars ... ibi**, "The same Mars ... there": A reference to a proverb about the general misery of war; see our note above at 199 and cf. Erasmus, *Adagia* 3649 = IV.7.49 **Mars communis**.

144. 565 **Quis hic furor ... accersere**, "What kind of madness ... mournful death?": A reference to the same phrase (with slightly different word order) in Lucan 1.681 **quis furor hic**. "Mournful": Latin has **atra**, "black", but "black death" would conjure notions of the bubonic plague that are not present here. Black was the color of mourning, so we elected to translate "mournful".

145. 566 **Imminet**, "stalking": "Stalking" maintains the metaphor of hostile movement here, but the Latin has **imminet**, which means more generally "threaten". There is a probable allusion to Cicero's *Tusculan Disputations* 5.62, the story of the sword of Damocles. There the sword is said to "hang over" (**imminari**; the same verb is used twice inside 4 lines) the young Damocles who is refered to as **adulescens inprovida aetate**, "young man of improvident youth", like our protagonist.

146. 571 **saniora**, "safer": In Latin **saniora** has connotations of both "healthier" and "smarter", and here it refers back to the discussion (lines 135-137) about being "sane" (**sanus**, the same word).

147. 574 **intermissam Palladem**, "interrupted studies": In the Latin "studies" is personified by a reference to **Pallas (Athena)**, the Greek goddess of practical smarts and wisdom.

148. 578 **dulce est praelium .. pueri instar sapit**, "likes battle ... less sense than a child": Here is another probable reference to Erasmus' famous tract "War is sweet (**dulce**) to the inexperienced" that is quoted verbatim in line 219. There is also some play with the notions of "wisdom" (**sapit**, "has sense") and "immaturity" (**instar pueri**, "like a child/boy").

149. 580 **Surdo fabula canitur**, "this story falls on deaf ears": "Telling a tale to the deaf" (the literal meaning of this phrase) was a common proverb in Latin. It is used in Terence, *Heautontimoroumenos* ("The Self-Tormenter") 222. The allusion is a double one, since Pontanus' play owes much to the laments of the father in Terence's play who has sent his son off to war. Erasmus also includes this proverb in his *Adagia*, **surdo fabulam narras**, meaning literally, "You are telling a story to a deaf person." (I.iv.87). We have translated the proverb here as the common American English phrase "this story falls on deaf ears."

150. 593 **Pietas iubet**, "Responsibility demands it": We translate **pietas** as "responsibility" here. This is most likely a reference to Vergil's *Aeneid*. The epic hero Aeneas is known chiefly for his **pietas** (loyalty and duty to the

gods, family, and the fatherland). Cf. *Aeneid* 2.750-798 (Verg. *Aen.* trans. Fagles 2.916-980): Aeneas leaves a besieged Troy and leads his family to safety. However, once outside the city walls, he discovers that his wife Creusa has fallen behind. Compelled by his sense of **pietas**, Aeneas rushes back to the city in search of his wife. He does not find her alive, but encounters her ghost, which dutifully accepts her fate and begs him to carry on with his destiny. Through Stratocles' speech, Pontanus connects Misomachus with Aeneas almost comically, which is all the more evident after the returning warrior does not receive the warm welcome he expects from his wife Faustina.

151. 595-7 **nihil ...improvisa**, "nothing ... wife": Note the irony in his mention of nothing being so "auspicious", **faustum**, which is the same root as in his wife's name, **Faustina** (see introduction above on names). Pontanus here makes general allusions to Homer's *Odyssey*, both to the return of Odysseus to the dutiful Penelope and also to other metaphors comparing Odysseus to a father coming home to his children. The following excerpt, which takes place as Odysseus comes ashore in Phaeacia, serves as an example (cf. Homer, *Odyssey* 5.392-399): "Joy...warm as the joy that children feel / when they see their father's life dawn again, / [after he's] lain on a sickbed racked with torment... / then what joy when the gods deliver him from his pains! / So warm, Odysseus' joy when he saw that shore..." (Trans. Robert Fagles, p. 164).

152. A4.1-2 **Complectendo ... potero**, "Hugs ... me": We bracket lines 1 through the first 2 words of line 2; these were inserted for the Mardi Gras performance of 1580, but when put here they are redundant with the immediately preceding line 602.

153. A.4.3 **faustitas mea**, "my fabulous fortune": **Faustitas** is an abstract noun related to Faustina's name. The root **faust-** means "blessed by good luck, fortunate, blessed". Faustina, as her remarks make clear, has been anything but fortunate since her husband's departure, and his referring to her as his "good fortune" is, at least in the short run, heavily ironic.

154. A4.4-5 **Iuno ... Jupiter**, "Juno ... Jupiter": Misomachus' attempts to flatter Faustina by calling her "Juno" (the wife of the chief god, Jupiter) parallel interactions in Plautus' *Amphitruo*. Disguised as Amphitryon, Jupiter deceives the general's wife Alcmena and has an affair with her which results in the birth of Hercules. Jupiter, incognito, charms his mistress saying, "But as to what you say, precious,—you oughtn't to be cross with me. / It was on the sly that I left my troops: this is a stolen treat, stolen for your sake... / I wouldn't have done such a thing, if I hadn't loved you with all my heart" (Plaut. *Amph.* 522-523; 525, Trans. Paul Nixon 1992 reprint.)

155. A4.8 **furcifer**, "bastard": The word **furcifer**, here translated as "bastard," is a derogatory term rarely used outside Plautine comedies (cf. *Amph.* 285, *Cas.* 139, *Mil.* 545). In line 563 of Plautus' *Captivi*, for example, the captive Aristophontes berates an old man named Hegio, **At etiam, furcifer, male loqui mi audes?** "But do you too, you lowlife, dare to bad mouth me?"

156. A4.16 **plus oculis te amarem**, "If I ... my own eyes": Classical lyric poets, especially Catullus and Sappho, commonly used the eyes as a metaphor for strong erotic desire and for the most precious of possessions. Cf. Catullus 3.5, describing a girl's affection for her pet, **quem plus illa oculis suis amabat**, "whom she used to love more than her own eyes." Cf. also Sappho's description of a woman with eyes like honey and worthy to be honored by Aphrodite, the goddess of erotic love (Sapph. 112.3-4).

157. A4.26 **non te agnosco**, "I do not recognize you": Here the word **agnosco** has resonances of official, statutory recognition, and the use of the negative implies a kind of legal rejection. A parallel usage of this legal term occurs in one of Pliny's letters to the emperor Trajan (Plin. *Ep.* 10.72). Pliny writes, "Certain persons have requested that cases concerning acknowledgment [**agnoscendis**] of children and granting of free-born rights to former slaves should come to me personally for settlement."

158. A4.39-40 **nec unum pilum ... Habes**, "every single hair ... worthless": Literally, "you do not have a single hair of a good man". A single hair, **pilum**, was a standard metaphor for something of very little significance. Cf. Catullus 17.17: **ludere hanc sinit ut lubet, nec pili facit uni**, "he allows her to play as she pleases, and he does not make [care] one hair". If hair is worthless, and even Misomachus's hair is no good, this is strong hyperbole for the extent of his incompetence.

159. A4.64-68 **miser ... calamitatibus**, "wretched ... suffering": There may be some humor in Misomachus' formulation of his situation, since it recalls lessons he learned in school: namely, rhetorical arrangement in groups of three, with each element more elaborate than its predecessor, and a sort of "scholastic" division of the problem into parts.

160. A4.70 **quarta ... furia**, "fourth fury": In Classical literature there were three canonical Furies, female spirits of implacable vengeance: Megaera, Tisiphone and Allecto (the last especially famous for her exploits in book seven of Vergil's *Aeneid*). Misomachus compares his wife to some of the most feared and repulsive female characters from ancient literature.

161. A4.71 **impatiens libidinis**, "unable to control their lust": The Latin is a bit difficult and more literally says: "the nature of women has grown

used to not putting up with (or enduring) desire." The phrase **impatiens libidinis** also appears in the preface of Servius' fourth century CE commentary on Vergil. Servius (whom Pontanus knew well) states that Vergil was retiring and modest to the point of getting the nickname "Virginal" (Parthenias). He then adds this sentence: "**Omni vita probatus uno tantum morbo laborabat; nam impatiens libidinis fuit**" "Through his entire life he had a good reputation, but suffered with just one affliction: for he was intolerant of sexual desire." Pontanus appears to have lifted this phrase from the famous commentary on Vergil and applied it to women. He was not the first; Poggio Bracciolini's collection of jokes has this phrase used of a woman: "**…cum opipare ventrem cibo potuque farsisset, mulier, libidinis impatiens, virum amplectitur, osculaturque…**" "…and when she had lavishly stuffed her stomach with food and drink, the woman, impatient of lust, embraced and kissed the man…"

The idea of a woman who is unable to control her sexual desires comes straight from the Classical tradition, and appears especially in humorous works. For instance, Ovid writes in his *Ars Amatoria* (1.277-278) **Conveniat maribus, nequam nos ante rogemus / Femina iam partes victa rogantis agat** "Should it suit us males not to ask any woman first, the woman, already won, would play the asker" (trans. J.H. Mozley, p. 33, slightly modified). Ovid is implying that women are even more eager for sexual encounters than men, and he then goes on to describe famous lustful women in mythology, such as Myrrha (285) and Pasiphae (295). Likewise, in his sixth satire, a famous invective against women, Juvenal writes about how Chastity has left this world in disgust because of the adulterous ways of women (1-24). Again, he gives examples of such women, such as Eppia, wife of the Emperor Claudius, who he claims was so insatiable that she secretly worked in a brothel to satisfy her lust (114-135). Likewise, Petronius famously writes in his *Satyricon* about the widow of Ephesus who is so lustful that she carries on an illicit affair with a soldier in her husband's very tomb (111-112). When Misomachus, then, says women are "**impatiens libidinis**," he is recapitulating this Roman comic tradition. In none of these Classical accounts, however, does the phrase **impatiens libidinis** occur; this is clearly from Servius.

162. A4.72-74 **Quid si ... det operam?**, "What if ... 'pay attention'?": This line is a reference to the affair between Vulcan's wife Venus and Mars the god of war. The most famous account is Homer, *Odyssey* 8.300-410; cf. also Ovid, *Metamorphoses*, 4.167-189. In the story, Mars and Venus are discovered **in flagrante delicto** in the house of Vulcan by the all-seeing sun god. Upon learning of the affair, Vulcan forges a net of bronze in which he ensnares the two lovers the next time they bed together (Ov. *Met.* 4.167-189). Misomachus' comparison is particularly apt because Vulcan himself is a blacksmith and thus similar to Misomachus the metalworker.

163. A4.75-77 **Arietem**, "battering ram": The term "battering ram" has a sexually charged meaning. Compare the male chorus in Aristophanes' *Lysistrata* who are metaphorically castrated when their battering ram and torches are destroyed by their female counterparts (Ar. *Lys.* 287-310). Similarly, this battering ram refers to an erect (but ineffective, in this context) phallus. The Roman army was skilled in siege warfare, and utilized rams to breach city walls. Roman authors used military vocabulary extensively to describe sexual conquests. In his *Amores*, Ovid says that all lovers are essentially soldiers between the sheets and describes making love as an army laying siege to and storming a fortified city (Ov. *Am.* 1.9.1-45).

164. A4.77-8 **mora ... iras ... implacabiles**, "delay ... implacable anger": Misomachus may here be referring to the "proverbial" delayer, Quintus Fabius. This general Fabius earned his epithet **Cunctator**, "the Delayer," during the Second Punic War when he faced the "raging and implacable anger" of Hannibal. Plutarch writes (*Life of Fabius Maximus* 5.1), "He [Fabius] did not purpose to fight out the issue with him [Hannibal], but wished, having plenty of time, money, and men, to wear out and consume gradually his culminating vigour, his scanty resources, and his small army." This strategy ultimately led to Hannibal's retreat and Rome's victory. If noticed, the allusion would be functional, for it would signal that Misomachus (true to his name) is moving from the besieger, who uses a battering ram (see previous note), to the besieged, who uses patience and delay (traditionally "female" tactics).

165. A4.80 **mea lux meaque salus**, "my light and salvation": Pontanus appears here to be making allusions to both Christian and pagan literature. Cf. *Vulgata* Psalm 26.1 (27.1): **Dominus lux mea et salutare meum** (other versions: **Dominus lux [illuminatio] mea et salutare meum**), "The lord is my light/illumination and my safety/salvation". Cf. also Plautus, *Captivi* 863-865: **Cui deorum?** Ergasilus: **Mi hercle, nam ego nunc tibi sum summus Iuppiter, idem ego sum Salus, Fortuna, Lux, Laetitia, Gaudium. proin tu deum hunc saturitate facias tranquillum tibi.** "Hegio: To what deity? Ergasilus: To me, by gad! For I'm your Jupiter Most High now, myself; and Salvation, Fortune, Light, Gladness, Joy—they're all this identical I! So mind you placate this divinity by stuffing him full" (trans. Nixon).

166. A4.84 **foedifragus**, "treacherously": **Foedifragus** is a rare word that literally means "breaker of treaties" and is most often used of treacherous enemies. The **–fragus** part means "breaker". **Foedus** has a range of meanings: formal treaty between states; private pact or contract; the marriage bond or other sexual union; a tie of kinship; a law of nature (see *OLD* **foedifragus**). Misomachus can claim to have violated almost all of these: his military contract, by desertion; the marriage and sexual bonds clearly; the kinship ties with his children; and he even mentions

his violation of the "law of nature" (A5.63).

167. A4.85-99: The dialogue between husband and wife is a parody of a confession conducted according to of the Catholic Sacrament of Penitence. The Council of Trent (1545-1563) had declared in its 14th Session: "Contrition, which holds the first place amongst the aforesaid acts of the penitent, is a sorrow of mind and a detestation for sin committed, with the purpose of not sinning in the future. This feeling of contrition was at all times necessary for obtaining the pardon of sins ... [T]his contrition implies not only an abstention from sin, and the resolution and beginning of a new life, but also a hatred of the old ..." The council further defined "imperfect contrition, which is called attrition, since it commonly arises either from the consideration of the heinousness of sin, or from the fear of hell and of punishment;" and declared that if regret "renouces the desire to sin and [it] hopes for pardon, it ... is even a gift of God and an impulse of the Holy Ghost..."

"It [the coucil] teaches furthermore, that the liberality of the divine munificence is so great that we are able through Jesus Christ to make satisfaction to God the Father not only by punishments voluntarily undertaken by ourselves to atone for sins, or by those imposed at the judgement of the priest (**sacerdotis arbitrio**) according to the measure of our offense (**delicti**), but also, and this is the greatest proof of love, by the temporal afflictions (**flagellis**) imposed by God and borne patiently by us."

Misomachus illustrates the concept of attrition (i.e., imperfect repentance), for he loathes the military life and fears his wife, who asks him whether he is ready to repent before God with the purpose of not sinning in the future (line 91); after that Misomachus admits to being subject to her will (**arbitrio** line 99) as though she were his confessor. See Gallemart, sessio XIV, cap. 4, p. 147; cap. 9, pp. 158 f. English from Schroeder, Fourteenth session, chapter 4, pp. 91 f. and chapter 9, pp. 98 f.

168. A4.89-90 **deum Testem appello**, "I call God as my witness": See our note above at 389 **Deus te servet**.

169. A4.94 **Ach**, "Oh": Here Pontanus inserts the German interjection "ach." This is the only German word in the text. Pontanus likely includes it here because it is appropriate to the light, farcical tone of this section. Perhaps it also indicates a sort of switch to the present, allowing the audience to identify with this particular scene.

170. A4.95-96 **fidem coles / Maritalem**, "You will honor marital fidelity?": **Colere**. This word has double meaning in the text. Faustina uses one meaning, "to cultivate," to demand the maintenance of marital fidelity. On the other hand, Faustina implies another meaning of the verb, "to plow," as a reference to sexual intercourse. Catullus uses similar language

in 62.55: **Multi illam agricolae, multi coluere iuvenci**, "Many farmers, many oxen (= young lovers) have tended [plowed] her." This poem is about the marriage of a maiden, and the agricultural vocabulary has obvious sexual connotations. Catullus himself may have been influenced by the earlier Greek dramatist Menander (ca. 343-291 BCE). In lines 842-843 of Menander's *Dyskolos*, the character Kallippides says to Gorgias, "I betrothe my daughter now, young man, to you to harvest lawful children" (Men. *Dys.* 842-843). This was the traditional vocabulary of a Greek marriage ceremony (Loraux 76). Page DuBois comments extensively on the metaphor when she discusses similar agricultural vocabulary used in *Oedipus Tyrannus*. She describes Jocasta as being "double ploughland," meaning that not only had she been "plowed" by Oedipus' father, but also by Oedipus himself (DuBois 77). The chorus laments: "How, O how, have the furrows ploughed / by your father endured to bear you?" (quoted from DuBois 77). The agricultural vocabulary itself conveys the ancient understanding of women as the earth and men as cultivators. Just as crops are generated from the earth, a child is generated from a woman's womb. In the ancient world, men owned their wives much as they did their fields, which they were responsible for tending (DuBois 65). In this line, therefore, Faustina is referencing antiquity's understanding and associated vocabulary of sexual intercourse and a man's marital duties.

171. A4.99 **arbitrio**, "control": The language here suggests a sexual role reversal. Customarily, the wife would have been under the "control" (**arbitrium**) of her husband; now, instead, Misomachus is submitting to his wife. This is done for comic effect, and to show just how emasculated Misomachus is here. In Pontanus' time, the word **arbitrium** primarily referred to the will, as in Erasmus' *De Libero Arbitrio*, or, *The Freedom of the Will*. **Arbitrium** is also used in confessional language: see our note on lines A4.85-99.

Decorative vignette from a 16th century print.

Appendices

Good students and bad students in *The School of Christ* and
The School of Satan from a booklet of moral examples, Munich 1618.

Appendix A

On Humanistic Schools and Humanistic Courses of Study in the Society of Jesus
Jacobus Pontanus

Five reasons why the Jesuits properly value, and should value, these studies:

I. They are the gateway for entry into the most powerful principalities. Through them we acquire the friendship of great princes. They recommend us highly to every class, the highest and the lowest, seeing that everyone desires to see his children distinguished and honored for their learning and religious devotion. Without this service people will be insufficiently appreciative of the rest of the things we do. Take away the schools — who then will look us straight in the eye?

II. Even if these studies cannot compete with others in dignity, they surpass them through enriching and passing on utility. Other disciplines are for a few; these are for the masses. Even among the well–educated you will find barely one in thirty who has arrived at a deep understanding of literature, since these are generally ranked with the priests and monks. Our humanism ranges far and wide among the whole human race and nurtures its seedlings throughout towns and principalities; it sows its seed, and we see and will see its rich and extensive harvest.

III. These studies are essentially ethical: whether you read an historian, poets, or an orator – in Greek or Latin – almost every single page presents an opportunity to promote virtue or to warn against vice – a thing that does not happen in physics, metaphysics, logic, and not even everywhere in theology. Although we strive for both ends we prefer making students good to making them learned. In a single one of your sermons from time to time you might succeed in bringing a usurer to give up usury, a whore–monger to stop whoring, and likewise with the remaining sins. However, a good teacher, if he accepts a boy still untainted by any vices, will, with constant encouragement and a kind of fatherly care, lead him away from those vices completely, like a judge, and will raise him toward a Christian life. The result is that the boy does not so much need to become good from bad; rather, he has no idea how to turn out bad from good and fears the bad vehemently. In this matter (i.e., moral progress) – just as in teaching letters – the second instructor follows the first, the third follows the second, the fourth follows the third, etc.

IV. From the spirit our studies learn respect, modesty and circumspection. In turn, from our studies the spirit learns attractiveness, wisdom and efficiency. All three are certainly important and necessary for skillful human interaction, but certainly seem to be expected rather more from the humanities than from other disciplines. The others are more strict, but the humanities are gentler and by far more suitable for general human affairs: hence their name.

V. Without the humanities the other studies grow cold and are in some way mute and dead. The humanities are their life, spirit, motion, blood and bone, without which all their splendor and dignity fades away.

MPSI vol. 7, mon. 12 III, pp. 93–94.

MVNDVM TRADIDIT DISPVTATIONI EORVM *Eccl. III.*

Title eines Ingolstädter Thesenzettels über das Sechstagewerk.
Stich von Wolfgang Kilian 1636 (²/₃).

Title page of a philosophy disputation Ingolstadt 1636 of Leodegard Hertenstein, S.J., with the globe and scientific instruments. Motto: "He hath set the world in their heart," which traditionally was understood to mean that God allowed humans to dispute about the natural world.

Appendix B

Pontanus on Writing Comedy

Introduction

Pontanus wrote a textbook on literary matters (*Poeticarum Institutionum Libri Tres*) that gives us a rich source of material about how he viewed comedy. The book covers writing across all genres, and the sections on drama are extensive.[1] A translation of the relevant passages would be far too long for a book of this scope. What follows, then, is a paraphrase of Pontanus' remarks on writing plays, especially comedies. We have selected passages that are particularly relevant to the characters and material found in *Stratocles*.

Pontanus' texbook is "scholastic" in nature, and thus exhibits a strong tendency to create and define categories and subcategories, with many examples for each. Most of the examples he cites are from the canonical Latin comic writers, Plautus and Terence. Little of what he says is original, and most of it is adapted from classical authors who write on literary criticism. The chief innovation of the Jesuits in this regard is the focus on Tragicomedy, a genre in which one could place

1. In the 1584 edition, the section on comedy comprises sections 12–17 of book 2, pages 88–108. Pontanus devotes thirty pages to epic and thirteen to tragedy.

the *Stratocles*. According to ancient literary theory, epic and tragedy contained characters that were greater than normal: gods, heroes (offspring of gods and mortals) and extraordinary humans. Comedy, on the other hand, is supposed to contain characters who are worse than normal: thieves, pimps, whores, con–men and tricky slaves, among others. Since Jesuit drama was self–consciously moralizing, it was necessary to introduce characters who were admirable in order to lift the moral tone of the play. Likewise, the lower–class characters and their pursuits and diction had to be cleaned up for the schoolboy audience. This softening of traditional comic material and the introduction of "good" characters from the more serious genres was a hallmark of Jesuit school drama. In *Stratocles*, the teacher Eubulus, although he has his foibles, speaks well and has his students' best interests at heart. Despite this mixing in of higher–register elements, however, the play remains "comic" because it has a happy ending, unlike the catastrophes in tragedy and the frequent sad elements in epic.[2]

Pontanus on Comedy: Highlights

Definition: Comedy is dramatic poetry that teaches the way humans generally act and thus imitates public and private actions. It also has verbal wit and jokes (89).

The Constituents of Comedy: There are four main elements: Plot, character, bon mots or memorable phrases, word choice or diction. These four are necessary and also found in tragedy; other elements are apparatus (staging and costuming) and melody (94).[3]

---

2. Pontanus 1584, ch. 12, 88–89. All subsequent references are to page numbers from this edition.
3. Pontanus' play is written in a basic dialogue meter, unlike the elaborate meters used in parts of tragedies (like arias in operas). Stratocles originated as a dialogue, and even in its later and more elaborate versions it is restrained in its staging. We have no unambiguous way of knowing, beyond a few stage directions and remarks made by other characters, what the scenery and costuming would have

How to write a comedy: First, think up a story, which is called the plot. It should be morally uplifting and accurately reflect the mores of different types of people. Memorable phrases are also important, since words reveal a person's inmost feelings and opinions. Proper word choice is also necessary (94–95).

Plot: Avoid miraculous events, since they belong to tragedy or epic. Use low–class characters and names to go with them.[4] One unified action is best, and should be completed within a few days at most. Coincidences or chance occurrences, especially ones that cause unexpected happiness or pain, are good. Plots can be simple, where there is no reversal of fortune or recognition of earlier misconception or wrongdoing. The complex plot, where there is reversal or recognition or both, is best.[5] The plot has two parts: the involvement or complication, and the resolution. The first leads to a conflict, and then after a change of attitude it proceeds to the end (96–97).

Jokes: Regardless of the kind of plot, jokes and funny situations turn up throughout, and the whole play should be spiced with wit. This is what constitutes comedy, just as pity and fear are proper in tragedy. It's necessary, however, to do this in a way that even censorious people won't object. Plautus was excellent at this. Avoid jokes or phrases that fall flat, those that have no zing, or ones that are overly vulgar.

Terence has fewer jokes, but he puts people on stage who are just like those in real life: people who are not so upright or wise that they can't make mistakes or be fooled or irritate others, but who at the same time are not unsympathetic.

---

been like, but the Jesuits in later times especially were known for elaborate sets and costumes. See Introduction on Jesuit theater.

4. See Introduction on names.

5. Note that Stratocles comes to see the error of his ways and returns to school, rejecting his earlier boasting. Similarly, the estranged husband and wife are reunited, with the soldier recognizing the error of his ways in going to war. The *Stratocles* is thus a good example of a complex plot.

頁

All the disagreements, arguments and slapstick should work toward a happy ending (96).

Character: Everything depends on whether a character is deserving of praise or blame, and whether certain acts or traits coincide with that character's station in life. For example, a lower–class man could play the oboe well and pride himself on it, but the same skill in a king is worthy of censure. A wife should sew and weave well, but that's a fault in a man. In short, different habits and customs work for different characters. It's important to conform to standard expectations when developing characters, and to make their words and conduct fit the inherited opinions of the majority of people (97–98).

Consistency is important: characters should be recognizably the same at the beginning and at the end, so long as the plot allows it. Everything should be kept as true to life or as believable as possible. Horace and Aristotle are the great authorities here, and observe that each stage of life has its own proper qualities:[6]

- Boys like to play with their friends, get angry quickly and then reconcile just as fast, and change mood hourly.
- Teenagers like to play outdoors with horses and dogs, are easily seduced into wrongdoing, are mean and rude to their teachers and authority figures, lack foresight, spend money too easily, are passionate and have high spirits, and change their interests quickly.
- Men have changed their interests: they work hard for wealth and influence, are slaves to earning distinction and very cautious about doing what will require more effort later.

6. Pontanus is here so indebted to Horace that he simply prints lines 156–174 of Horace's *Art of Poetry*. Note the similarity of the material here to, e.g., Eubulus' speech on the failings of youth in lines 331–337. Pontanus is sufficiently familiar with this work that he puts line 169, with slight changes, in the character Faustina's mouth at *Stratocles* A4.12–13.

- Old men have lots of troubles: they're miserly and
  greedy, cold, fearful, slow, sluggish, greedy for
  life but short on hope, hard to deal with, fond of
  complaints, apt to praise the time when *they* were
  boys, and fierce critics of the young (98–99).

Memorable phrases: It's best if these appropriately express the character's essence. Since comic characters are not of the highest sort, these phrases should not be too lofty or grandiloquent. Big philosophical questions or elaborate eulogies should be avoided. Everything should be kept moderate (100).

Word choice: Comedy doesn't reach for tragedy's loftiness, but also doesn't sink to what's vulgar. It should be easy, understandable, pleasant, standard, elegant and simple, with only a bit of ornament, and not too grand. Sometimes the rhetoric will rise when a character gets angry, but everything should be kept within sensible bounds. Always reflect common attitudes; proverbs are great for this (100).

Scenery and Costumes: Old men should wear white, which is traditional. Teenagers can wear purple or multicolored clothes, for this will reflect their changeable nature. Soldiers should wear military overcoats and a dagger or sword. Happy characters should wear light colors, sad or unlucky ones should wear dark and tattered garments. Married women and down–on–their luck females should wear black. Prostitutes should wear something dirty, to reflect their greed (100–101).

SCHOLA DIABOLI. 247

Hæc est Gens quæ non audiuit vocem Domini
Dei sui. nec recepit Disciplinam. Hierem. 7

**Schulbild aus dem Alphabetum Diaboli
1618.** Stich von Raph. Sadeler (¹/₁).

Good students and bad students in *The School of Christ* and
The School of Satan from a booklet of moral examples, Munich 1618.

Appendix C

Renaissance School Hazing

Introduction

We include this appendix in order to supply some context for Stratocles' remarks about the harshness of school life. His complaints seem grossly exaggerated, and indeed they are when compared with the privations, indignities and violence of life on campaign. Nonetheless, life at school for boys in the sixteenth century was physically challenging and often humiliating in ways not adequately understood by contemporary students.[1] This humiliation and injury was often supported and even administered by the institutions themselves.

A particularly clear illustration of this is a ritual common in European schools called "Deposition." This name is shorthand for **Depositio Cornuum**, a ritual "removal" or "setting aside" of "horns." These "horns" were viewed as symbols of animality and immaturity (like antlers that are shed), and incoming students had them "removed" as part of their enrollment. The new students were called **Beani**, "Beanies." The name is commonly derived

1. Pontanus discusses flogging as part of school life in three of his *Progymnasmata*: 21, 25, 58.

from the French "bec jaune" or "yellow beak", i.e., an immature bird.[2] This development worked in the following way: **bec jaune** becomes **beanus**, likely pronounced "bay–ah–nus". The English "greenhorn" is similar, along with (at least in meaning) the old cowboy designation of the neophyte as "tenderfoot."[3] The ritual involved dressing incoming students as animals and then having the bestial part of them removed and "polished" and their bodies "cleaned" (more on this below) as preparation for their new life in the academy. They were subject to physical and mental tests and then told how they were to view these rites as making them ready for their studies. The ritual lasted in some form from the eleventh to the eighteenth century, and appears to have been introduced into Germany, where Pontanus was active, in the fifteenth century.

There is almost no scholarship on this aspect of European academic life in English, aside from a Wikipedia entry, which is helpful for its bibliography (sources almost entirely in German) and links to images of the various implements, actions and practices involved.[4] What follows is a very short description of the rite;[5] then a translation of a kind of instruction manual from a Jesuit school for someone overseeing the process (usually the head of the Philosophy faculty); then some short excerpts from Pontanus' own *Progymnasma* 84, a dialogue between an older and a younger student who discuss the ritual. To our knowledge these last two are translated into English here for the first time.[6]

2. We know of no source that connects this term with the practice common in American universities nearly a century ago of having newly matriculated male students wear small brimless caps called "beanies". The similarity is striking, however.

3. We possess an entire play called Beani that was most probably written by Pontanus; it focuses on new students in need of education generally and not so much on the ritual of deposition. This piece is included in M5, the manuscript that also contains the Faustina sections of Stratocles that were included for a Mardi Gras performance (see Introduction on text history).

4. See Leinsle 2006, 263–269 for a clear discussion and relevant bibliography.

5. http://en.wikipedia.org/wiki/Deposition_%28university%29

6. This brief description is based primarily on Füssel and Fabricius. Füssel in particular is recent and gives very full bibliographical help. He also delves into questions of the origin and symbolism of various aspects of the rite.

Short Description of Ritual of Deposition

There are of course both local and temporal variations, but certain features of the ritual remained largely constant. New students were dressed with costumes that included oversized representations of animal attributes, usually horns and boar's teeth. After being herded into a central place and addressed in a body, groups of them were then led off for removal of these attributes, usually with special oversized implements like pliers, grindstones or axes. Some German universities still retain the instruments.[7] During the assembly and after, the older students reviled the newcomers as animals. Often further tormenting of the "Beanies" would ensue; they would be measured and "finished" or "polished" by older students wielding woodworking implements (e.g., planes and rasps). They would then be ritually cleaned up; beards would be painted on and then "shaven", and their hair pulled and cut. The cleansing included cleaning the ears of wax with ear spoons, so the potential for lasting harm was real if excessive physical force was used.[8] Anyone familiar with the capacity for cruelty of adolescent males will know that injuries and abuses were common. These were increasingly guarded against with ever more stringent sanctions, until in the nineteenth century the rituals were largely discarded. Until then, however, physical abuse and humiliation were common.

In addition to the above, students were given riddles or read Latin that they could not understand and were laughed at for their confusion. Toward the end of the ritual the "salt of wisdom" would be put in their mouths, or the "wine of joy" poured over their heads; one can easily imagine the excesses to which these parts of the ritual could be taken. The Beanies were forced to swear an oath never to attempt to exact revenge on their tormentors for their maltreatment, and often a significant sum of money was exacted, part of which often went to defray the

7. There are interesting links in the web address noted above that take one to images of these at places like Leipzig.
8. Cleaning the ears of wax was a common part of personal grooming in the Renaissance, and a small spoon or pick for it was an implement regularly found among the personal possessions of the middle class.

costs of a large party that followed the rite. At the end the Dean of the school would declare them free of their "Beanism", i.e., their immaturity, and pronounce them fit to enter the academy. The following year they would participate in the humiliation of the new class.

Instructions for Deposition [9]

1.1 The master "remover" (=hazer or initiator) will have the names of those to be initiated memorized, and all of these right at the beginning of the hazing will be presented by two of his associates and on bended knee will seek initiation from the chief hazer himself.

2. The initiator will pose these questions to the initiands:
    1. Are all of you prepared to endure patiently whatever you will have to endure in this hazing rite?
    2. Do you promise total obedience in this proceeding to me, the hazer, and to my masters, my associate hazers?
    3. Have you been prepared to throw off all lack of polish and sophistication in your conduct and to really learn the life that is worthy of a well-born, free and academic man?

When they respond by nodding to these questions, they will be warned that no one is to leave prior to the hazing of each and every one. Then those who are to be led to the hazing rite itself will be dismissed from the hazing site by clearly defined squadrons.

3. Depending on the large or small size of those to be initiated, more or fewer will be led forth for hazing, and to each one of them the initiators will do the following:

---

9. Beránek 25–35; we rely on his numbering scheme and his text, pp. 29–31, which contains no apparatus criticus and has a few errors that are here corrected silently. The original is from the Czech state archive in Prague, manuscript CXXIII/2, folios 1–2. The rhetoric is fairly clipped and formal, like an instruction manual written by a haughty superior.

1. They will take the horns off each one.
2. They will paint the face with a black color to look like a beard.
3. With a plumb line or string they will measure them lying on the ground at the same time, or five or three at a time.
4. After standing them up in the same place they will hack, slice and cut them, paying attention to them all, so that they do not seriously injure or mangle someone; especially for those who are younger or quicker to anger they should take care to maintain moderation.
5. After they have been ordered to rise and then sit down they will pluck and cut their hair, pull out a tooth and scrub their tongue.
6. They will clean out their ears.
7. They will be able to work them over with some literary questions, while keeping in mind each one's talent and nature.

4. After they have done things like this with one squadron, they will dismiss it before leading in the next group right away, and then the next, for putting them to the test likewise.

5. When everyone has been readied for action in the way just described, finally, just as in the beginning, all at the same time will be presented to the chief hazer. Since they are changing their attitudes publicly in a way that befits them, he will conduct an examination of them from a board on which the students' symbol is depicted, concluding with an explanation of the symbol.

6. "And so, because up to this point you 'beanies' do not know the real life of a free and well–born man, that is, of a good student and an academic, understand these things that have been done to you:

    a. Your horns have been removed so that you understand,

before everything else, that all mental stubbornness and unsophisticated roughness must be put aside. It is no doubt proper for a studious young man to be malleable and to follow the lead of the teacher who is forming and teaching him.

b. We have painted beards on you to advise you through this ritual that from here forward you ought to present yourselves as *men*, if not in years, then certainly with a thoroughly mature character, having rejected boyish frivolity and lack of restraint for a serious and proper mode of conduct.

c. Forcing you to our norms and rules we have beaten, excised and amputated whatever seemed idiotic or deformed, to show you that you ought to align your life and character to the standard of academic laws and practices, so that there is nothing in you that could justifiably offend anyone.

d. We have plucked out and shorn your hair so that you recognize that womanish softness in care for the body or coiffure is a terrible disgrace for a student; we will not allow someone who claims to be a scion of Minerva to walk around like some slut for Venus.

e. We pulled out your tooth and purified your tongue in this ceremony while exhorting you to refrain from the malicious bite of bad reputation, from unbridled freedom of speech and from lust, and to remember how things stand in the presence of an educated man: young fellow, it is scarcely the case that you get to speak in your own behalf. In crowds act as if you are uninformed, and where your elders are present, do not say much, and good will will attend you in proportion to your respectful conduct.

f. We cleaned your ears, which contain the sense of discipline, so that, since you have poured into this university for the sake of learning the liberal arts, you may be tireless in listening to those subjects and diligent in learning them. That is how to avoid what the master used to say, that in the theater 'stone sits on top of stone' or 'whoever has left his country after being maimed, let him return in the same way he had left it'."[10]

7. When they have been readied he will give them the salt of wisdom with these, or with similar, words: "So, since you have been initiated by these rituals as genuine seekers of learning and wisdom and have been taught all that is respectable in character, take the salt of wisdom, and first and foremost see to it that, spicing all your words and deeds with the salt of wisdom and moderation, you prove yourselves to be genuine seekers of wisdom and real students of the liberal arts.

8. "Finally, this one thing remains: I absolve you of your Beanism and proclaim you free men. Therefore let this redound to the glory of God the Greatest and Best, and to the honor of the perpetual Virgin, equal to God, and to the honor and distinction of this your alma mater, and to the benefit and distinction of all of you. I am teacher of the X arts and of philosophy, and in this university X, I, who eagerly cultivate the authority of the esteemed rector and master of this university, pronounce you who are present here as those who have been trained by academic ceremonies and rites to establish a life worthy of a free–born and liberally educated academic. I absolve you, since you have been freed from Beanism, and I pronounce you absolved in this very academic gathering. You are to be enrolled in the lists of this and of other universities and shall enjoy academic privileges and freedoms. In the name of the Father, Son and Holy Spirit, Amen."

10. Both of these appear to be proverbial phrases relating to stupid or uneducated people who have been untouched by learning or experience. Pontanus refers to the former in the sixth note to his second *Progymnasma* in a similar context about the wisdom or utility of educating children. He attributes this phrase to Aristippus and says it is found in Aristotle. Aristippus said that if he educates his son, at least in the theater one stone would not sit atop another. Ancient theaters were made of stone; the implication is that the student should learn more than the seats when he hears lectures, that he not remain uninfluenced by what he hears.

Dialogue on Hazing

Pontanus, *Progymnasma* 84, **Depositio**, or Hazing ("Putting Aside the Horns of Immaturity")

In this dialogue the younger student Narcissus complains bitterly about the terrible abuse and insults he suffered during his "deposition". The older student Gulielmus listens without much sympathy and reminds him that others have suffered the same or worse. Here we see Pontanus using a typical bit of student life as the subject of one of his early exercises in Latin style and usage.

This translation is less formal than the rhetoric of the original, and is slightly abridged. Particularly strained jokes or repartee that is not very descriptive have been left out, and the gaps are indicated by ellipsis marks (...).

Characters: Narcissus and Gulielmus

NARCISSUS

The first, the first of April! No day will ever erase your memory from my mind. I'd have happily gouged my eyes out that day, it brought me so much moaning and trouble. One thing's for sure; it'll go down on my calendar as a black day...

GULIELMUS

... What's the reason you're so angry about today that you swear you'll remember it forever?

NARCISSUS

Because today I suffered terribly.

---

11. The "aside" is not indicated in the original, but it makes sense if this were a "performed" text, especially since such asides were common in Roman comedy, and Pontanus often includes tropes and conventions from that genre in his Latin exercises.

GULIELMUS

...You suffered awfully? What was it, please? *(aside)* Although I think I've figured things out already.[11]

NARCISSUS

Are you clueless what notice was posted on the school's front doors?

GULIELMUS

Do you mean the harsh decree that Bedellus the headmaster always used when giving orders to the Beanies? The one that said they had to assemble at noon in the appointed place, ready to hear and endure whatever the law and fairness demanded?

NARCISSUS

I'm telling you, that that damn edict brought me outrageous pain.

GULIELMUS

I'll tell you right out what I think: I figure nothing unusual or nasty happened to you beyond what's happened to others.

NARCISSUS

Immortal God! If everyone is enrolled like this, you're more likely, as far as I see it, to create donkey–drivers or cattlemen than students. But anyway, they handled my fellow students more gently.

GULIELMUS
I don't believe it.

NARCISSUS
But I believe it, since I saw it with my own eyes and I felt it. They picked me out just like some wild animal standing in front of them, and then after just about everyone else was sent off they went after me like hunters with their dogs ... As soon as I entered, someone greeted me as Chief Beanie, and others responded with sneers, a few gave me the finger, and finally everyone surrounded me and taunted me, like birds mobbing an owl. Right then and there my heart leapt into my throat in terror ... I was forced to lie spread–eagled on the ground and to stay there motionless, like a corpse.

GULIELMUS
What happened to you then?

NARCISSUS
I was worked over nicely with builder's tools just like some hunk of timber for a construction site: a saw, axe, pick and double–headed hatchet. They hammered my legs as much as they wanted, and my arms and sides – why mince words? – my whole frame. That's why it's no wonder if I look thinner than yesterday or the day before: I lost a lot of "wood" from myself when they trimmed off the "twigs."

GULIELMUS
Three years ago in the very same workshop I saw awful goings–on, and I was a big part of them.

NARCISSUS

They shaved off my beard, good barbers that they are, although so far I'm completely beardless, and they washed my head with cold water that they made me bring out from the kitchen myself in a dirty copper bucket. The meanest guy, whenever he came up beside me, kept splashing my face with his hands out of this bucket, and he laid me low with a bash to the knee. After that they combed me with a comb so fine you'd think it was a garden rake ... What should I say about the towel they used to dry me off? It was soft as a rake and gentle as lye...

GULIELMUS

How I wish I'd been there for that comedy!

NARCISSUS

It wasn't a comedy, it was torture ... Ah, how everything hurts; how I was yanked, smashed and pulverized. But then (and this is unspeakable), in return for these insults and humiliation, as if I had deserved them, I had to pay out I don't know how much cash, to thank them, and to recite a formal, solemn oath that I won't ever try to avenge myself. If I hadn't said that, I could now barely keep myself from "returning the favor" to a few of the ones who were a little more thorough in badgering me. I've never been through anything nastier.

GULIELMUS

Whatever was done wasn't done out of ill–will or hatred, but for fun and to get people laughing. Let it go, and remember that others up to this point have suffered likewise or will do so in the future.

NARCISSUS

You're asking for something awfully difficult. On top of that, listen to this nice little trick. They put in front of us an inkbottle made on a lathe, along with a pen and paper: they ordered us to write something literary. When I wanted to open up the bottle, I couldn't, since in fact it didn't have a stopper that could be removed. The whole thing was one solid piece ... At this point some guy jumps up and bashes my fingers with a stick, saying, "By the gods above, this Beanie hasn't even learned how to open an ink bottle!" Everyone laughed ... I tell you, my fists are itching to get at him.

GULIELMUS

You got very gentle treatment there – ha ha ha ... Is there anything else like this that happened?

NARCISSUS

Some bastard put something in my travel bag without my knowledge. ... It was a letter, as if sent by my mother, which he read openly to everyone after he pulled it out. Good God, what was worse? How hard and mean they laughed, or how many were laughing, both on their own and because the others were laughing?

GULIELMUS

What was in the letter?

NARCISSUS

My mother kept lamenting my absence and giving me women's compliments – that is, really stupid ones – reminding me how much pain she endured in giving me birth, how diligently she had breast-fed me, how often she had kissed her beautiful baby, how carefully she raised me, how devotedly she cherished me right from my very first years just as if I were her own heart, how I had been the apple of her eye, her little kiddy–poo, her lamby–wamby, her fuzzy chicky, and sweeter than honey. Then she added that she hadn't been able to sleep, and that she kept weeping harder every single day because of the torments she had heard I was likely to suffer in this hazing ritual. They jeered that they had thought the whole thing up and written it down. The whole time they thought they'd never done anything funnier. How they almost fell over with laughing! How they brandished the letter in front of me! How they hit me with their fists! ... If I had known this was about to happen, I would have gone away to a school where nothing like this happens...

BIBLIOGRAPHY

Works by Jacobus Pontanus
In chronological order

Rochus Perusinus. *De scribenda et rescribenda epistola liber.* Ed. Jacobus Pontanus. Dillingen: Mayer, 1578.

Pontanus S.J., Jacobus. *Progymnasmatum Latinitatis (…) volumen primum (-tertium).* Ingolstadt: Sartorius 1588; 16th edition Dilingen: Bencard/Federle, 1684.

Pontanus S.J., Jacobus. *Poeticarum institutionum libri tres: eiusdem tyrocinium poeticum.* Ingolstadt: Sartorius 1594; 3rd edition Ingolstadt: Sartorius, 1600 [contains *Stratocles*]; Excerpts in: Johannes Buchler. *Thesaurvs phrasivm poëticarvm.* Adjecta est *Institutio poëtica* ex R.P. Iacobi Pontani S.I libris desumpta, musarum tironibus necessaria. Amsterdam: Ravensteinius, 1665.

Pontanus S.J., Jacobus. *Floridorum libri octo.* Augsburg: Ad Insigne Pinus 1595.

Pontanus S.J., Jacobus. *Symbolarum libri XVII : Quibus P. Virgilii Maronis Bucolica, Georgica, Aeneis: ex probatissimis auctoris declarantur, comparantur, illustrantur.* Augsburg: Praetorius/ Ad insigne Pinus, 1599 (Reprint: New York: Garland, 1976); Lyon: Pillehotte, 1604.

Vergil. *Pvblii Virgilii Maronis Poetarum Latinorum principis opera indubitata omnia.* Ed. Jacobus Pontanus. Cologne: Gualterus: 1604, 2 vols.; Sedani: Iaonnon, 1625; 1628.

Philippus Solitarius. *Dioptra.* Transl. by Iacobus Pontanus. Ingolstadt: Sartorius 1604.

Pontanus S.J., Jacobus. *Colloquiorum sacrorum libri quatuor (...).* Augsburg: [no publisher] 1609; Ingolstadt: Sartorius, 1610.

Pontanus S.J., Jacobus. *In P. Ovidii Nasonis ... Tristium, et De Ponto libros novi Commentarii.* Ingolstadt: Sartorius, 1610.

Ovid. *Metamorphoseōn Liber XV. Sectionibus, et in easdem argumentis probe distinctus, & locupletatus.* Commentary by Jacobus Pontanus. Munich: Hertsroy, 1613; Antwerp: Nutius, 1618 (Reprint: New York: Garland, 1976); Antwerp: Meursius, 1647.

Pontanus S.J., Jacobus. *Attica Bellaria.* 3 vols. Munich: Hertsroy, 1616-1620; Augsburg: Apergerus 1617; Frankfurt: Schönwetter/Humm, 1644.

Pontanus S.J., Jacobus. *Ethicorvm Ovidianorvm Libri Qvatvor.* Munich: Hertsroy/Ingolstadt: Angermaier, 1617.

Pontanus S.J., Jacobus. Φιλοκαλία *sive excerptorum e sacris, et externis auctoribus.* Augsburg: Apergerus, 1626.

Ioannis Cantacuzeni Eximperatoris Historiarum libri IV. Ed. Ludovicus Schopenus. Preface by Jacobus Pontanus S.J. Bonn: Weber, 1828-1832.

Theophylacti Simocattae Historiarum libri octo, ed Immanuel Bekker. Bonn: Weber, 1834; transl. and preface by Jacobus Pontanus [also: ed. Charles Annibal Fabrot, Venice: Iavarina, 1729].

Beránek, Karel. "Beánie v Klementinum," in *Pocta Dr. Emmě Urbánkové. Spolupracovníci a pártele k 70 narozeninám.* Prague: Státní Knihovna, 1979, pp. 25-34; contains edition of *Ritus et ordo depositionis* that was probably authored by Pontanus (see our translation in Appendix C).

Pontanus S.J., Jacobus. "Stratocles sive Bellum/Stratocles oder Der Krieg," in Fidel Rädle , ed. *Lateinische Ordensdramen des XVI. Jarhrhunderts mit deutschen Übersetzungen.* Berlin:

de Gruyter, 1979, pp. 296-365, 556-562, 593-596.

Pontanus S.J., Jacobus. "Dialogus de Connubii Miseriis," ed. Fidel Rädle, in Joseph P. Strelka, ed. *Virtus et Fortuna. Festschrift für Hans-Gert Roloff*. Berne: Lang, 1983, pp. 290-314.

Nonnulli circa studia humaniora tractatus, MPSI 7, Mon. 12, pp. 88-104 (pp. 93 f., section III: *De studiis et scholis humanioribus Societatis Iesu* is translated in this book; see our Appendix A).

Oeconomia dialogicae scriptionis, MPSI 6, Mon. 31, pp. 473-475.

Secondary and Other Sources
In alphabetical order

Alszeghy, Zsoltné, and Katalin Czibula, Imre Varga, eds. *Jezsuita iskoladrámák* [Jesuit School Dramas], Régi Magyar Drámai Emlékek, XVIII. Század, vol. 4/I. Budapest: Argumentum-Akadémiai Kiadó, 1992.

Antoninus Florentinus. *Summae Sacrae Theologiae, Iuris Pontificij, & Caesarei*. Venice: Iunta, 1571.

Arriaga, Rodericus de. *Disputationes theologicae in Secundam Secundae D. Thomae: Universi Cursus Theologii tomus quintus*. Antwerp: Plantin/Moretus, 1649.

Augustine. *Letters*. Trans. John Leinenweber. Liguori, Mo.: Triumph Books, 1992.

Backer, Aloys de, and Carlos Sommervogel. *Bibliothèque de la Compagnie de Jésus*. Brussels/Paris: Schepens, 1895 ff. [On Pontanus: vol. 9, col. 779; Suppl. col. 712 f.].

Barsby, John, ed. *Terence: Eunuchus*. Cambridge: Cambridge University Press, 2008.

Bauer, Barbara. "Jakob Pontanus SJ, ein oberdeutscher Lipsius," *Zeitschrift für Bayerische Landesgeschichte* 47 (1984): 77-120.

Bauer, Barbara. *Jesuitische ars rhetorica im Zeitalter der Glaubenskämpfe*. Frankfurt: Lang, 1986.

Behringer, Wolfgang. *Witchcraft Persecutions in Bavaria: Popular Magic, Religious Zealotry, and Reason of State in Early Modern Europe*. Cambridge and New York: Cambridge University Press, 1997.

Bielmann, Joseph. "Die Dramentheorie und Dramendichtung des Jakobus Pontanus S.J. (1542-1624)," *Literaturwissenschaftliches Jahrbuch der Görres-Gesellschaft* 3 (1928): 45-85.

Bielmann, Joseph. „Die Lyrik des Jakobus Pontanus S.J., "*Literaturwissenschaftliches Jahrbuch der Görres-Gesellschaft*" 4 (1929): 83-103.

Binder, Wilhelm. *Novus Thesaurus Adagiorum Latinorum: Lateinischer Sprichwörterschatz*. Stuttgart: E. Fischbacher, 1861.

Blum, Paul Richard. "Jacobus Pontanus SJ," in Stephan Füssel, ed. *Deutsche Dichter der Frühen Neuzeit*. Berlin: Schmidt, 1993, pp. 626-635.

Boehm, Letitia. "Die Erneuerung des Augsburger Schulwesens im 16. Jahrhundert: christliche Pädagogik in konfessioneller Parität," *Stephania* 54 (1982): 39-54.

Bremer, Heinrich S.J. "Das Gutachten des P. Jakob Pontan S.J. über die humanistischen Studien in den deutschen Jesuitenschulen (1593)," *Zeitschrift fur Katholische Theologie* 28 (1904): 621-631.

Broedel, Hans Peter. *The Malleus Maleficarum and the Construction of Witchcraft: Theology and Popular Belief*. Manchester, New York : Manchester University Press, 2003.

Cajetan, Thomas de Vio. *Summula*. Venice: de Lenis, 1581.

Drummond, Robert Blackley. *Erasmus: His Life and Character as Shown in His Correspondence and Works*. London: Smith, Elder, & Co., 1873.

DuBois, Page. *Sowing the Body: Psychoanalysis and Ancient Representations of Women*. Chicago: University of Chicago Press, 1988.

Duhr, Bernhard. *Geschichte der Jesuiten in den Ländern deutscher Zunge*. 4 vols. Freiburg: Herder/Munich-Regensburg:

Manz, 1907-1928 [On Pontanus: vol. I, pp. 200-205, 280-287, 671-673; vol. II.1, p. 503; vol. II.2, pp. 369 f., 440; vol. III, p. 379].

Dürrwächter, Anton. "Aus der Frühzeit des Jesuitendramas," *Jahrbuch des Historischen Vereins Dillingen* 9 (1896): 1-54.

Erasmus, Desiderius. *Collected Works of Erasmus, Vol. 9*. Trans. R.A.B. Mynors. Annotated by James M. Estes. Toronto: University of Toronto Press, 1989.

Erasmus, Desiderius. *Collected Works of Erasmus, Vol. 35*. Trans. Denis L. Drysdall. Ed. John N. Gant. Toronto: University of Toronto Press, 2005.

Erasmus, Desiderius. *Collected Works of Erasmus, Vol. 36*. Trans. John N. Grant, Betty I. Knott. Ed. John N. Gant. Toronto: University of Toronto Press, 2006.

Erasmus, Desiderius. *Collected Works of Erasmus, Vol. 64*. Trans. Emily Kearns, Caroline White, Michael J. Heath. Ed. Dominic Baker-Smith. Toronto: University of Toronto Press, 2005.

Erasmus, Desiderius. *The Complaint of Peace*. New York: Cosimo, Inc., 2004.

Erasmus, Desiderius. *Erasmus: The Education of a Christian Prince with the Panegyric for Archduke Philip of Austria*. Ed. Lisa Jardine. Cambridge: Cambridge University Press, 1997.

Erasmus, Desiderius. *Opera Omnia*. Amsterdam: North Holland Publishing Company, 1969 ff.

Erasmus, Desiderius. *The Praise of Folly*. Trans. H. H. Hudson. Princeton: Princeton University Press, 1941.

Flemming, Willi. *Geschichte des Jesuitentheaters in den Landen deutscher Zunge*. Berlin: Selbstverlag der Gesellschaft für Theatergeschichte, 1923 [On Pontanus: pp. 4, 97, 107, 126, 155, 223, 249, 256, 285, 300].

Fumaroli, Marc. "Aspects de l'humanisme Jesuite au Début du XVIIe Siècle," *Revue des Sciences Humaines* 40 (1975): 251-268.

Fumaroli, Marc. "Une pédagogie de la parole: Les *Progymnasmata latinitatis* du P. Jacobus Pontanus," in P. Tuynman et al. eds. *Acta Conventus Neolatini Amstelodamensis.* Munich: Fink,1979, pp. 410-425.

Gallemart, Joannes, ed. *Sacrosanctum Concilium Tridentinum.* Cologne: Busaeus, 1688.

Gerl, Herbert. *Catalogus Generalis Provinciae Germaniae Superioris et Bavariae Societatis Jesu 1556-1773.* Munich: Oberdeutsche Provinz S.J., 1968 [On Pontanus: p. 322].

Grubb, Judith E.. *Women and the Law in the Roman Empire: A Sourcebook on Marriage, Divorce and Widowhood.* London and New York: Routledge, 2002.

Harnack, Adolf von. *Militia Christi: The Christian Religion and the Military in the First Three Centuries.* Philadelphia: Fortress Press, 1981.

Harris, Stephen L., and Gloria Platzner. *Classical Mythology: Images and Insights.* 4th ed. New York: McGraw Hill, 2001.

Homer. *The Odyssey.* Trans. Robert Fagles. Penguin: New York, 1999.

Ignatius, of Loyola, Saint. *Ignatius of Loyola: the Spiritual exercises and selected works.* Paulist Press: New York, 1991.

Janssen, Johannes. *History of the German People.* London: Kegan Paul, Trench, Trubner & Co. Ltd, 1906 [On Pontanus: vol. 9, pp. 321, 373; vol. 13, pp. 137, 160, 384, 394].

Koch, Ludwig. *Jesuiten-Lexikon.* Paderborn: Bonifacius-Druckerei, 1934 [On Pontanus: vol. 2., p. 1453 f.].

Kosch, Wilhelm. *Deutsches Literatur-Lexikon.* Berne/Stuttgart: Francke, 1990 [On Pontanus: vol. 12, col. 168 f.].

Kovacsóczy, Farkas. *De administratione Transylvaniae dialogus,* Claudiopoli (now Cluj in Romania) 1584. Full text available at web site of the Hungarian Academy of Sciences, http://www.hik.hu/tankonyvtar/site/books/b151/ch27s01.html

Kroess, Alois. *Geschichte der Böhmischen Provinz der Gesellschaft Jesu.* Wien: Opitz, 1910.

Juvencius, Joseph. *Magistris scholarum inferiorum Societatis Jesu De ratione discendi & docendi ex decreto Congregat. Generalis XIV.* Cordoba: Crespus 1753.

Lagerlund, Henrik. "Medieval Theories of the Syllogism, *The Stanford Encyclopedia of Philosophy* (Spring 2004 Edition). Ed. Edward N. Zalta. Stanford: The Metaphysics Research Lab, 2004.

Lefkowitz, Mary. *The Lives of the Greek Poets*. Baltimore: Johns Hopkins University Press, 1981.

Leinsle, Ulrich G. "Werke Jacob Pontanus' in der Handschrift Studienbibliothek Dillingen XV 399," *Jahrbuch des Historischen Vereins Dillingen* 106 (2005): 87-146 [On *Stratocles*: pp. 132-135].

Leinsle, Ulrich G., "Dichtungen Jacob Pontanus in der Handschrift Studienbibliothek Dillingen XV 399," *Jahrbuch des Historischen Vereins Dillingen* 107 (2006): 259-323.

Leinsle, Ulrich G. *Dilinganae disputationes: Der Lehrinhalt der gedruckten Disputationen an der Philosophischen Fakultät der Universität Dillingen 1555-1648*, Regensburg: Schnell + Steiner, 2006 [On Pontanus: pp. 79-85, 481-485, and *passim*].

Leinsle, Ulrich G., "Jacobus Pontanus SJ (1542-1626), Humanismus und *pietas* in der Spätrenaissance," *Beiträge zur Geschichte des Bistums Regensburg* 43 (2009): 81-99.

Lukács, Ladislaus, ed. *Monumenta Paedagogica Societatis Iesu*. 5 vols. Rome: Institutum Historicum S. I., 1965-1992 (*Monumenta Historica Societatis Iesu*, vols. 92, 107-108, 124, 129, 140-141).

Mahlmann-Bauer, Barbara. "Pontanus, Jacob," *Neue Deutsche Biographie*, vol. 20, Berlin: Duncker & Humblot, 2001, p. 616.

Martial. *Epigrams*. Trans. D. R. Shackleton Bailey. Cambridge, Mass: Harvard University Press, 1993.

McCabe, William H. *An Introduction to the Jesuit Theater: A Posthumous Work*. St. Louis: Institute of Jesuit Sources, 1983.

Nessler, Nicolaus. *Dramaturgie der Jesuiten Pontanus, Donatus und Masenius. Ein Beitrag zur Technik des Schuldramas*. Brixen, Germany: Programm des Gymnasiums zu Brixen,

1905, p. 2-48.

Ovid. *The Art of Love, and Other Poems*. Trans. J. H. Mozley. Cambridge: Harvard University Press, 1979 (2nd ed., rev. by G. P. Goold).

Pachtler, G. M., ed. *Ratio Studiorum et Institutiones Scholasticae Societatis Jesu per Germaniam olim vigentes*. Berlin, 1887-1894.

Padberg, John W., ed. *The Constitutions of the Society of Jesus and Their Complimentary Norms*. Saint Louis: The Institute of Jesuit Sources, 1996.

Pavur, Claude, trans. *The Ratio Studiorum. The Official Plan for Jesuit Education*. Saint Louis: Institute of Jesuit Sources, 2005.

Pelzel, Franz Martin. *Boehmische, Maehrische und Schlesische Gelehrte und Schriftsteller aus dem Orden der Jesuiten von Angang der Gesellschaft bis auf gegenwaertige Zeit*. Prague: Im Verlag des Verfassers, 1786 [On Pontanus: p. 4-7].

Plautus, T. Maccius. *Comedies*. Trans. Paul Nixon. The Loeb Classical Library. Cambridge: Harvard University Press, 1992 (reprint).

Polgár, László. *Bibliographie sur l'historie de la Compagnie de Jésus*. Vol. 4: *Les personnes*. Rome: Institutum Historicum S. I., 1990 [On Pontanus: p. 688].

Possevino, Antonio. *Il Soldato Christiano con l'instruttione dei capi dello essercito catolico. Libro necessario a chi desidera sapere i mezzi per acquistar vittoria contra heretici turchi, et altri infedeli*. Rome: Dorici, 1569.

Possevinus, Antonius. *Bibliotheca selecta qua agitur de ratione studiorum*. Rome: Typographia Apostolica, 1593.

Rädle, Fidel. "Aus der Frühzeit des Jesuitentheaters: Zur Begleitung einer Edition lateinischer Ordensdramen," *Daphnis* 7 (1978): 448-452.

Riley, Henry Thomas, trans. *The Comedies of Plautus*. vol. 2. London: G. Bell and Sons, 1912.

Schings, Hans-Jürgen. "Consolatio Tragoediae, Zur Theorie des barocken Trauerspiels," in Reinhold Grimm, ed. *Deutsche*

Dramentheorien I. Wiesbaden: Athenaion, 1980, pp. 19-55.

Schroeder, H. J., ed. *Canons and Decrees of the Council of Trent.* St. Louis/London: Herder, 1941.

Sifakis, G. M. *Aristotle on the Function of Tragic Poetry.* Herakleion: Crete University Press, 2001.

Specht, Thomas. *Geschichte der Universität Dillingen.* Freiburg: Herder, 1902.

Suárez, Franciscus. *Commentariorum et disputationum in Tertiam Partem Divi Thomae, tomus secundus.* Venice: Minima Societas, 1594.

Suárez, Francisco. *Selections from Three Works of Francisco Suárez, S.J.: De Legibus, Ac Deo Legislatore, 1612; Defensio Fidei Catholicae, Et Apostolicae Adversus Anglicanae Sectae Errores, 1613; De Triplici Virtute Theologica, Fide, Spe, Et Charitate, 1621.* Ed. Gladys L. Williams and Henry Davis. (*The classics of international law,* no. 20). Oxford: Clarendon Press, 1944.

Szarota, Elida Maria, ed. *Das Jesuitendrama im deutschen Sprachgebiet: eine Periochen-Edition: Texte und Kommentare.* Munich: Fink, 1979-1987, 7 vols.

Toletus, Franciscus. *In Summam Theologiae S. Thomae Aquinatis Enarratio,* ed. Iosephus Paria, vol. 2. Rome: Congregatio de Propaganda Fide, 1869.

Treggiari, Susan. *Roman Marriage: Iusti Coniuges From the Time of Cicero to the Time of Ulpian.* Oxford: Oxford University Press, 1991.

Valentin, Jean-Marie. *Le théâtre des Jésuites dans les pays de langue allemande (1554-1680).* Berne: Lang, 1978 [On Pontanus: vol. I, p. 480-488; vol. III. p. 1157-1161, 1473–1474].

Valentin, Jean-Marie. *Le théâtre des Jésuites dans les pays de langue allemande: répertoire chronologique des pièces représentées et des documents conservés (1555-1773).* Stuttgart: Hiersemann, 1983-1984 [On Pontanus: pp. 1097 f., 1205].

Valentin, Jean-Marie. *Theatrum Catholicum. Les Jésuites et la scène en allemagne au XVIe et au XVIIe siècles.* Nancy: Presses Universitaires, 1990 [On Pontanus: p. 214].

Valentin, Jean-Marie. *Les Jésuites et le théâtre (1554-1680)*. Paris: Desjonquères, 2001 [On Pontanus: pp. 281-289].

Vitoria, Francisco de. *Political Writings*. Ed. Anthony Pagden and Jeremy Lawrence. Cambridge: University Press, 1991.

Wang, Andreas. *Der "miles christianus" im 16. und 17. Jahrhundert und seine mittelalterliche Tradition: Ein Beitrag zum Verhältnis von sprachlicher und graphischer Bildlichkeit*. Berne: Lang, 1975.

About the Aperio Series

Aperio: I uncover, disclose, make accessible

Through "Aperio Series: Loyola Humane Texts," Loyola University Maryland's Apprentice House publishes important and illuminating texts in the Humanities that have been edited, annotated, and/or translated by the College's students in collaboration with faculty. Students also work with faculty to design and publish the texts. The texts are intended for all readers but should be of particular interest and use to college students and in undergraduate classes.

The future of publishing...today!

Apprentice House is the country's only campus-based, student-staffed book publishing company. Directed by professors and industry professionals, it is a nonprofit activity of the Communication Department at Loyola University Maryland.

Using state-of-the-art technology and an experiential learning model of education, Apprentice House publishes books in untraditional ways. This dual responsibility as publishers and educators creates an unprecedented collaborative environment among faculty and students, while teaching tomorrow's editors, designers, and marketers.

Outside of class, progress on book projects is carried forth by the AH Book Publishing Club, a co-curricular campus organization supported by Loyola University Maryland's Office of Student Activities.

Student Project Team for *Soldier or Scholar*:
    Kevin King '09
    Amanda Merson '10
    Andrew Zaleski, '11

To learn more about Apprentice House books or to obtain submission guidelines, please visit us online: www.ApprenticeHouse.com.

Apprentice House
Communication Department
Loyola University Maryland
4501 N. Charles Street
Baltimore, MD 21210
Ph: 410-617-5265 • Fax: 410-617-5040
info@apprenticehouse.com

CPSIA information can be obtained
at www.ICGtesting.com
Printed in the USA
LVOW03s0127260717
542657LV00001B/10/P